Index of
Resources

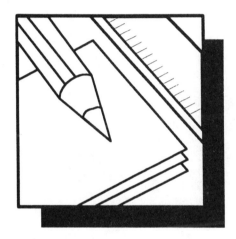

TABLE OF CONTENTS

I.
The Resume

Table of Contents

FUNCTIONAL / COMPUTER OPERATIONS

NAME
Address • Telephone

SUMMARY

Computer operator with six years varied experience at major electronics firm.

- IBM PS2 Model 30 experience
- Ten years experience with high-speed close tolerance machinery.
- Troubleshooting on coating equipment and pod machines using pressurized systems.

SELECTED ACCOMPLISHMENTS

COMPUTER EXPERIENCE

- Received hands-on and classroom training in the use of an IBM PS2 Model 30, with 3 1/2" disk drive and 20 meg. drive, Hayes 2 modem, mouse, IBM Pro-printer, Microsoft windows with word processor and graphics capability. Personally own above model.
- Performed numerical and statistical data entry in a research and development environment.
- Trained in MultiMate word processing and Lotus 1-2-3.

HIGH-SPEED CLOSE TOLERANCE EQUIPMENT

- Built sub-assembly parts with tolerances to within a thousandth of an inch. Monitored process using quality control procedures.
- Troubleshot problems as needed on machinery. Results: Higher yields and run time.
- Maintained a machine log accounting for all mechanical and electrical down-time and material losses. Results: More efficient planning of workload and machine use.

MOTIVATION AND PRODUCTIVITY

- Assessed and evaluated needs prior to start of shift to insure proper shift efficiency.
- Ten-year record of perfect attendance.

WORK EXPERIENCE

ABC CORPORATION, Nashua, NH   **1986 - Present**
Computer Operator

RIVERSIDE AMUSEMENT PARK, Agawam, MA   **1984 - 1986**
Ride Operator

COLUMBIA BICYCLE MANUFACTURING, Westfield, MA   **1982 - 1984**
Production Worker

NAME   **PAGE TWO**

EDUCATION

Greenfield Community College, Greenfield, MA, 1982 - 1984, Course: Media Technology

Specialized Company-Sponsored Training:

Lotus 1-2-3, Entry-level
Intro to MultiMate Advantage 2
Basic Computer Skills (IBM PS2 Model 30)

Graduate, Lakeland High School, Chicago, IL

CHRONOLOGICAL /FINANCE

NAME

Address • Telephone

SUMMARY

Over 12 years Senior Executive experience, progressing to VP/Controller with high technology engineering/manufacturing companies selling commercial and military products internationally. Solid background in international licensing, negotiation, business acquisition, production, distribution, accounting and credit. Outstanding leadership skills in developing, implementing and tracking company business and MIS strategies that foster team work, continuous improvement, and shareholder value.

PROFESSIONAL EXPERIENCE

PTI TECHNOLOGIES INC., Newbury Park, GA   **1991 - 1996**
Vice President of Finance

Responsibilities:

Directed staff of 3 responsible for financial administration, management information, and telecommunications systems.

Accomplishments:

- Spun off the company by establishing stand alone business systems. Developed business plan to grow sales to $90 million; sold company to investors for a $19 million premium.
- Implemented new product investment strategy by licensing foreign technology, acquiring key personnel, investing $5 million in manufacturing equipment and facilities, and purchasing a UK filter manufacturer/distributor for $8 million, to grow sales by $30 million at a 62% margin.
- Protected $6 million in business from price erosion by establishing customer long-term agreements to lock in prices and hedged profit risks by negotiating supplier contracts.
- Led MIS staff to employ network technology and analysis efforts to design systems meeting value-added and customer-driven requirements, reducing staff 27% over 3 years, hard copy reports by 40%, and avoiding $120,000 in computer upgrades.

TELEDYNE SYSTEMS COMPANY, Northridge, CA   **1988 - 1991**
Controller

Responsibilities:

Directed staff of 34 responsible for all Financial Administration.

Accomplishments:

- Improved ROI 38% by coordinating the merger of three companies, eliminating redundant and non-value added work, adopting best practices, training staff, and delegating responsibilities.
- Negotiated with customer representatives over $2 million in price increase by presenting persuasive cost justifications and applying knowledge of contract terms and conditions.

NAME   **PAGE TWO**

HUGHES AIRCRAFT COMPANY, El Segundo, CA   **1982 -1988**
Group Manager of Financial Planning/Systems/Auditing

Responsibilities:

Directed 18 staff members responsible for strategic planning, budgeting, reporting, investment analysis, financial systems, audits and special investigative work for Corporate Executives.

Accomplishments:

- Implemented planning and reporting process at $1.3 billion in sales organization which fostered management teamwork to improve profits 13%.
- Lead analysis teams that recommended equipment purchases, facilities reductions, favorable tax positions, organizational structure changes, and financial system and procedure changes to executive staff to facilitate an 11 headcount reduction.

PRICE WATERHOUSE, Los Angeles, CA   **1978 - 1982**
Senior Auditor

Responsibilities:

Managed and performed financial audits, SEC filings, and business acquisitions analysis for manufacturing, engineering, and service oriented companies.

Accomplishments:

- Improved consulting services and reduced cost an average of 20% by analyzing client's businesses, customizing audit approaches and applying innovative PC technology.
- Provided over $1 Million in client billings by promoting and improving the firm's capability to service the needs of companies performing long-term contracts.

EDUCATION

LOYOLA MARYMOUNT UNIVERSITY OF L.A., Bachelor of Science   **1976**

PROFESSIONAL DEVELOPMENT

CPA, State of California

SEMINARS

Total Quality Management Certification • General Supervision • Team Building

ASSOCIATIONS

American Institute of CPA's • California Institute of CPA's

FUNCTIONAL /HUMAN RESOURCES

Name

Address • Telephone

BUSINESS SUMMARY

Over 10 years as a Human Resource professional in the financial services industry. A catalyst, problem solver, and coach for organizations around the world with a flair for recognizing opportunities, selling new ideas, and starting up new Human Resource functions. Special depth in organization development, management training, recruiting and career development. An energetic, innovative professional who has a sense of team, cares about people, and produces results.

SELECTED ACCOMPLISHMENTS

- Sold the concept of management training to a major bank for the first time in its history, and trained 1,800 middle and top managers in performance feedback and problem solving.

- Guided middle management groups through corporate power game simulations and led them through the self-discovery process in a respectful, supportive way, resulting in greater awareness and willingness to strengthen less developed capabilities.

- Established the first career path for high potential operations management trainees in a top insurance firm.

- Consulted to management and labor of a major bank on successfully changing the profile, internal structure, and culture of a core business group to reflect its new business strategy.

- Launched a merchant bank's first major strategic recruitment campaign at top-ten schools across the country (graduate business schools and liberal arts colleges) to capture 25 percent more candidates in a faster time frame.

- Elicited a standing ovation as a guest speaker for Wesleyan University's panel on "Changing Careers."

BUSINESS HISTORY

STV COMMERCIAL BANK & TRUST, New York, NY.   **1983 - 1995**

Manager (Vice President):   1988 - 1995

- College Relations & Recruiting
- Operations Management Recruiting
- Human Resource System: Asia/Pacific
- Corporate Human Resource Development

Manager of Training (Assistant Vice President)   1983 - 1987

NAME

TOP LINE INSURANCE, Short Hills, NJ.   **1981 - 1983**
Training Specialist, Underwriting & Sales Training

PRIORITY TRUST COMPANY, New York, NY   **1979 - 1981**
Supervisor, Clerical Training Programs
Supervisor, Operations

ABC MANUFACTURING, INC., Orange, NJ   **1978 - 1979**
Procedural Writer, Systems

EDUCATION

COLUMBIA UNIVERSITY, Masters of Arts, 1987
Concentration: Organizational Psychology & Consulting

OHIO UNIVERSITY, Bachelor of Arts, 1978
Major: Psychology. Minor: English

SPECIAL COURSES

Productive Conflict, National Training Laboratories, Decision & Problem-Solving Analysis,
Wilderness Survival Training, Vision Quest

CHRONOLOGICAL/INFORMATION SYSTEMS

NAME
Address ♦ Telephone

SUMMARY

Ten years extensive data communications experience including four years managing and maintaining a Novell Netware 250 node, 7 server WAN utilizing token ring, ethernet, frame relay, and a DEC VAX 4000500. Expertise with IBM mainframe and midrange connectivity, T-1 circuits, personal computer and network hardware, and most DOS/Windows applications. Exceptional troubleshooting, training and documentation skills.

TECHNICAL SKILLS

HARDWARE:	PCs, network cards, MAUs, local and remote bridges, routers, DSU/CSUs, muxes, terminal servers, cluster controllers, protocol converters, and printers.
SOFTWARE:	MS Windows/Office/Access, Lotus Notes/cc:Mail/1-2-3, Word Perfect (DOS/Windows), and most widely used business applications.
CABLING:	Unshielded twister pair, RS-232, Ethernet, coax, and twinax
OPERATING SYSTEMS:	DOS, Novell, Netware, VMS, OS/2, CICS
PROTOCOLS:	IPX, TCP/IP, LAT, SNA/SDLC, BSC

PROFESSIONAL EXPERIENCE

ANDREWS CORPORATION, Torrance, CA   **1984 - 1994**

LAN Manager   1991 - 1994

- ♦ Maintained and expanded Novell Netware 386 LAN/WAN with virtually no downtime, resulting in an increase in overall employee productivity and improved communication.

- ♦ Facilitated conversion of printed business forms to laser-printed forms, saving thousands of dollars per month in printing costs.

- ♦ Implemented Lotus Notes server for evaluation of a Helpdesk database, consolidating Technical Support information from all sites onto a standardized wide area platform.

- ♦ Converted dial-up e-mail and leased lines to WAN, saving $50K per year in telecommunication costs.

- ♦ Absorbed network maintenance workload from sister site, saving $50K per year in additional salary expense.

Name

Page 2

Manager New System Development   1988 - 1991

Responsible for new systems, major enhancements to existing systems, budget of $4.0 million and supervision of 40 professionals. Key management programs and business systems were:

- Directed the implementation of an Advertising and Promotion Accounting System, which supported cost control (IBM 3084, IMS DB, COBOL)
- Directed the implementation of a distributed processing Total Maintenance System at 13 plants, reducing inventory costs by $1.0 million and increasing production uptime (IBM 8100, DMS, COBOL)
- Directed the implementation of a Retail Distribution Information System, which increased productivity and resulted in more effective advertising and a 20% improvement in out-of-stock conditions (IBM 3084, Telxon 701, COBOL, TECAL)
- Directed the implementation of a Financial Planning System that resulted in more effective pricing decisions (IBM 3084, IBM PC<, IFPS)
- Directed the implementation of Office Automation Systems that increased productivity 20% (IBM 3084, IBM S36, DEC Vax, Wang VS, IBM PC, SNA, DW4, Lotus)

Supervisor, Systems and Programming   1987 - 1988

Lead Analyst/Programmer   1984 - 1986

SHARED COMMUNICATIONS - Cincinnati, OH   **1980 - 1983**

Computer service bureau. Functioned as account sales manager.

DONLIN CORPORATION - St. Louis, MO   **1979 - 1980**

An international aircraft manufacturer. Functioned as a systems analyst/programmer.

EDUCATION

MBA, Finance, Xavier University   1980

BA, Math/Physics, Western Illinois University   1974

CHRONOLOGICAL/MANAGEMENT/CONTRACTS

NAME
Address
Telephone

SUMMARY

Contracts Manager with extensive experience in complex business transactions, contracts, negotiations, software/hardware licensing agreements, procurement and project management. A unique blend of legal and business experience with an outstanding record of sound business judgment, expanding responsibility and achievement across multiple functions. An excellent teacher and communicator. Builds a solid, highly motivated team.

EMPLOYMENT HISTORY

SCIENCE INSTRUMENTS COMPANY, Little Rock, AR   **1990 - Present**
Manager, Contracts

Provide business support, contract management and procurement of supplies and services for the Information Engineering Facility with $500M in annual sales. Principal negotiator with the authority to bind the corporation. Supervise contract administration, program planning and financial management for multi-year contracts. Develop and review proposal data for major programs. Resolve contractual and audit disputes.

♦ Negotiated numerous complex corporate Software Licensing Agreements with Fortune 100 Companies.

♦ Developed business practices and contracts for the Federal Sales Group which grew in annual sales of software and services from $500K to $35M.

♦ Ensured the legal protection of intellectual property and proprietary data.

♦ Negotiated a $350M Proposal with EDS to support the Department of Defense.

♦ Captured several targeted programs with an initial combined value of $125M by executing Strategic Alliance Agreements and Teaming Agreements.

♦ Received "Top Performer" Award 1993.

♦ Negotiated a Joint Development and Marketing Agreement with ABC Corporation.

♦ Negotiated a Software Distribution Agreement with INC.

NAME

GENERAL DEFENSE COMPANY, Barstow, CA   **1988 - 1990**
Financial Manager

Responsible for contract administration, financial management and pricing functions for five large contracts.   Managed operating trends by preparing and analyzing financial reports involving revenue, expense and schedule variations.

Supervisor, Contract Administration   **1986 - 1988**

Supervised contract administration function, proposals and change orders for a large government contract.

SPACE TECHNOLOGY, INC., Houston, TX   **1984 - 1986**
Attorney, NASA Contracts

Responsible for contract compliance, change orders and modifications for a large NASA contract with an Award Fee and Incentive Fee structure.

US ARMED FORCES   **1976 - 1981**
Captain, Combat Control Team

Leader of a Combat Team that conducted special operations for the Military Airlift Command.

EDUCATION

CALIFORNIA WESTERN SCHOOL OF LAW, 1984
Juris Doctorate

WEBSTER UNIVERSITY, 1978
Masters of Arts

BAYLOR UNIVERSITY, 1975
Bachelor of Arts

ASSOCIATIONS

AMERICAN BAR ASSOCIATION
FEDERAL BAR ASSOCIATION
UTAH STATE BAR ASSOCIATION
NATIONAL CONTRACT MANAGERS ASSOCIATION

NAME

ADDRESS • TELEPHONE

SUMMARY

Extensive business experience developed from close contact with leading executives from area companies in the furtherance of company objectives. Provided internal leadership in formulating policy, strategy, budgeting and marketing initiatives. Positions held required frequent interface with board members and senior staff from companies. Special skills also include:

- Project Management
- Business Development
- Community Relations
- Public Policy

PROFESSIONAL EXPERIENCE

CHARITIES SOUTH, Austin TX   **1980 - 1995**
Vice President

Responsible for the management of an annual budget of $1.85 million, a staff of 28, and a volunteer structure of over 20,000 in an area wide resource development program that produced $425 million for community programs and services.

- Provided professional staff support to CEO's and senior management.
- Staffed the only combined effort of community cooperation in resource development between Dallas and Ft. Worth.
- Established community relations by expanding proactive programs like customer service support, employee assistance programs, and recognition programs on a local and national level.
- Developed an on-the-job training module for staff that resulted in the successful completion of a $40 million project in less than 9 months.
- Developed and directed corporate development program that annually provided 8-10% increases.
- Coordinated with community planning agency for development of program/agency audits and community needs assessments.
- Developed and negotiated contracts for staff services and consultation with five other divisions.
- Staffed multiple boards of directors and committees.
- Created a position for the organization in the face of changing legislation to be the only legally defined organization to manage a program that gave the organization control of marketing, and planning and resource distribution.
- Improved a national program that provided for recognition of Fortune 500 companies for their community involvement.

NAME

CHARITIES SOUTH, Austin TX   **1977 - 1980**
Director

Planned, developed and staffed various processes in the areas of administration, training, special projects and policy development. Managed 26% of the resource development effort that provided $25 million. Provided for agency, media, and public relations. Managed 15 staff and 75 loaned executives.

- Developed corporate case presentation book that produced 12-16% annual increases in resource development production.
- Developed and implemented a wage/salary administration program.
- Co-chaired a multi-ethic task force that developed a community service program subsequently integrated into several agencies' programs.
- Analyzed and simplified organizational systems and procedures.

WORLD DISASTER RELIEF   **1970 - 1977**
Director

Responsible for disaster preparedness and relief efforts for 75 counties along the Texas Gulf Coast. Supervised and managed a professional and volunteer staff of up to 90 on various relief efforts. Directed programs on 18 major relief operations with expenditures of over 95 million.
- Established and directed the plan to provide relief efforts that included survey of needs, budget, staffing, financial management, supplies and staff support facilities.
- Prepared and managed both annual and project budgets.
- Provided services to a multi-cultural population.
- Developed and maintained liaisons with federal, state, local and military officials to implement an effective, timely response to customer needs.

MILITARY SERVICE   **1966 - 1970**

Honorably discharged after forty-five months of active duty. Served as an aircraft commander and instructor pilot in flight units in southeast Asia and the United States. Assignments included tour in the flight unit that supports the White House and the Pentagon.

COMMUNITY ACTIVITIES

BOY SCOUTS OF AMERICA
Serve as assistant scoutmaster and associate advisor to Order of the Arrow Chapter.
Member Cross Timbers District Committee, Boy Scouts of America
Chaired Steering Committee for community wide Friends of Scouting annual campaign that resulted in a 105% increase.

EDUCATION

UNIVERSITY OF TEXAS ARLINGTON

CHRONOLOGICAL/MARKETING

NAME
ADDRESS ♦ TELEPHONE

CAREER SUMMARY

Marketing/business development executive with national /international experience in industrial and consumer products companies. Proven initiator and strategic thinker with effective leadership, analytical, organizational and communication skills.

PROFESSIONAL EXPERIENCE

AVERY DENNISON - $2.5 Billion Corporation   **1984 - 1995**

Marketing Manager - Industrial Products Division, Azusa, CA   1988 - 1995
Managed a $37 million custom and stock data processing supplies business, reporting to the General Manager.

- ♦ Launched new products, wrote strategic plan, and directed all marketing projects.
- ♦ Set sales direction, supported field activities, and developed key account programs, increasing sales revenue by 12% over three years.
- ♦ Managed technical team, pricing, sales promotion and product management functions.
- ♦ Restructured a $12 million business segment, saving the Corporation $1.5 million net income.

Senior Product Manager - Consumer Products Division, Covina, CA   1987 - 1988

- ♦ Developed and executed promotions, introduced major new products and managed merchandising, advertising and pricing.
- ♦ Conceptualized and executed 2 major promotions, boosting sales by 50%.

Product Manager - Consumer Products Division, Covina, CA   1985 - 1987
Executed marketing plan for "Avery Notes", the first major competitor to the 3M Post-It-Note.

- ♦ Directed creative process for collateral, media, training tools, point-of-purchase merchandisers and consumer promotions.
- ♦ Executed four major regional roll-outs and conducted key accounts presentations, closing 4 of 5 major distributors.

Assistant Product Manager - Consumer Products Division, Covina, CA   1984 - 1985
Assisted in management of a $60 million consumer products division.

- ♦ Rolled out line extensions, developed new channels, and managed marketing budget of $1.4 million.

I - 13

Export Product Manager - Consumer Products Division, Covina, CA   1984 - 1985
Scope of responsibility included starting up an export business and documenting policies and procedures.

♦ Grew the business to $1 million in one year via direct mail and worldwide telemarketing.

IBM CORPORATION

Marketing Support Assistant, IBM Corporation, Phoenix, Arizona   1983 - 1984
Outside sales of typewriter, copier, word-processing and supplies lines to national accounts.

♦ Presented capabilities, negotiated contracts, closed sales.
♦ Set a national selling record for all IBM interns.

COCA-COLA

Assistant Market Analyst, Coca-Cola Bottling Company of Los Angeles, CA   1983
Created and coordinated the Hispanic marketing program for Los Angeles.

♦ Forecasted sales, developed promotions, organized special events.
♦ Assisted with regional introduction of Diet Coke.

EDUCATION

Master of International Management
American Graduate School of International Management, Glendale, AZ, 1984

Specialization: Marketing and Spanish.

Bachelor of Arts (with Honors), University of California, Santa Barbara, 1982

Specialization: Political Science and International Politics.

Junior Year in Spain, University of Madrid, 1980 - 1981

HONORS AND AWARDS

Guest Speaker, UCLA Women in Business Program, Los Angeles, 1986 - Present

Guest Lecturer, Department of Marketing, California State University, Los Angeles

FUNCTIONAL/MARKETING SUPPORT

NAME

Address | Telephone

SUMMARY

Thirty years diversified experience and success in marketing and technical service for a "Fortune 10" company. Strengths include:

- Direct Marketing
- Client Relationships
- Marketing Programs/Support
- Market-Driven Quality
- Project Management
- Information Systems
- Strategy Development
- Field Service Support

ACCOMPLISHMENTS

- Provided consulting and marketing services for Information Systems physical solutions. Expertise in the areas of data center construction and site fit-up, connectivity, relocation, environmental equipment and client end-user service and support.

- Exceeded sales projections consistently while maintaining high customer satisfaction levels. Attained 131% of 1992 quota, resulting in revenue flow of $7.2 million.

- Participated in nationwide task force to build services and support skills into marketable offerings and capabilities.

- Developed and marketed hardware and software services support business for the Los Angeles Public Sector client base; brought this start-up capability into a profitable posture by exceeding yearly revenue target.

- Developed, instituted and managed a client service request screening process, resulting in an increase in field personnel utilization and a measurable improvement in client satisfaction.

EMPLOYMENT

IBM, Los Angeles, CA   **1965 - 1995**
Advisor Services Marketing Representative

MILITARY U.S. ARMY SIGNAL CORP.   **1963 - 1965**
Specialist 4th Grade, Honorable Discharge

EDUCATION AND TRAINING

CITRUS COLLEGE, Associates Degree
Concentration: Industrial Management

BROOKLYN POLYTECHNIC INSTITUTE, Engineering Major

U.S. ARMY SIGNAL SCHOOL,
Concentration: Cryptographics

IBM,
Technical and Professional Development Classes

CHRONOLOGICAL/OFFICE ADMINISTRATION: DATA ENTRY

Name
Address
Telephone

SUMMARY

More than 15 years experience as a Data Entry Operator in the financial services industry. Strengths include accuracy, speed and attention to detail. Typing speed 60 words per minute.

EXPERIENCE

FIRST BANK, Sacramento, CA   **1979 - 1994**
Senior Clerical Specialist, Glendale, CA   1992 - 1994

Responsibilities:

Responsible for processing redemption certificates and clearing outstanding items for aging.

Accomplishments:

- Processed up to 50 redemption items daily, ensuring that all certificates were canceled and forwarded to the Records Center.
- Monitored print-outs of previous day's work and identified/corrected errors ensuring accurate processing of batches each day.
- Reviewed aging reports for prior year's transaction, researched and cleared $76 million outstanding items in 50 accounts.
- Assumed all supervisory duties in the Manager's absence, trained 4 temporary employees on Sunstar accounting system. Created a "tally-sheet" form, used to record and track completed unprocessed work.
- Received merit award for outstanding performance and dedication.

Senior Data Entry Technician   1987 - 1992

Responsibilities:

Input bonds and coupons on IBM Bondmaster System; researched and resolved duplicate coupon problems, assisted with logging batches, checked unposted batches, made reversals and repays, assisted Team Leader as needed.

Accomplishments:

- Researched and corrected 200 rejected items each day.
- Demonstrated flexibility by working long overtime hours as needed while maintaining accuracy and efficiency.
- Tracked and assigned bond numbers, ensuring accurate sequential order before printing.

Sub-Unit Supervisor

1979 - 1987

Responsibilities:

Supervised eight to nine employees in the Stock Transfer Section.

Accomplishment:

- Input of stop transfers on DAC Systems, reconciliation of computer print-outs requiring corrections to be sent out on computer rejects.

PROFESSIONAL DEVELOPMENT

Labor Relations   1980

Pre-Supervisory Workshop   1979

Banking People   1971

CHRONOLOGICAL/OFFICE ADMINISTRATION: EXECUTIVE SUPPORT

NAME
ADDRESS • TELEPHONE

SUMMARY

A Corporate Administrative Assistant / Executive Secretary with extensive experience at the highest executive level. Major strengths in organization and detail, verbal and written communication skills and all aspects of personalized travel arrangements. Exercise exceptional judgment and works independently. A well-organized, dependable professional who takes pride in her work.

PROFESSIONAL EXPERIENCE

WESTERN SECURITIES, Sacramento, CA   **1968 - 1992**
Corporate Administrative Assistant   1981 - 1992

Responsibilities:

Performed full range of secretarial and administrative support; drafted and prepared correspondence; managed extensive domestic/international travel arrangements; maintained complex business/social calendar; screened/answered mail and telephone calls; handled personal bookkeeping/recordkeeping; supervised other executive secretaries.

Accomplishments:

- Developed and coordinated detailed domestic and international travel itinerary for CEO and provided all necessary information related to scheduled business appointments and social events, significantly improving executive's productivity.

- Managed, organized, and distributed the full range of incoming executive correspondence. Made decisions on destinations and actions required on most items, releasing CEO for more important activities.

- Created a form that executives used to track business expenses more efficiently, expediting preparation of a final summary and ultimate reimbursement.

- Skillfully coordinated and dealt with the resolution of as many as 2 executive level customer complaints per week. Made decisions on appropriate solutions and action required to resolve issues originally targeted at the CEO.

- Developed and provided executives a daily and weekly computerized summary of business and social appointments.

- Coordinated meetings and appointments which frequently included regulators and major corporate clients.

NAME

Senior Secretary, Fiduciary Services Group   1978 - 1981

Responsibilities:

Provided secretarial support to Division Heads and Officers of Trust Marketing and Trust Real Estate Management Divisions.

Accomplishments:

- Complete payroll reporting and processing for 10-30 management employees with 100% accuracy.
- Easily handled a high volume of dictation work for head of Trust Real Estate Management Division, at levels up to 120 words per minute.
- Managed telephone contacts, correspondence, various reports, customer complaints, mail, meeting arrangements, and other appointments.

Secretary, Southern Division   1968 - 1978

Responsibilities:

Provided secretarial support to Regional Vice President, who supervised approximately branches, along with other officers on his staff. Very heavy dictation and typing of internal memoranda and reports, handled customer complaints, mail, and telephones.

EDUCATION

PASADENA CITY COLLEGE,
Concentration: Business

MARY'S BUSINESS HIGH SCHOOL, Diploma
Concentration: Business

PROFESSIONAL DEVELOPMENT

GLENDALE COLLEGE,
Concentration: Lotus 1-2-3, Microsoft Windows 3.1, Advanced Word Perfect 5.1

SPECIAL SKILLS

Word Perfect 5.1
Typing - 60 wpm
Gregg Shorthand - 100 wpm
DictaTelephone Capable

FUNCTIONAL/OFFICE ADMINISTRATION: OPERATIONS

Name
Address
Telephone

SUMMARY

A seasoned professional with 16 years experience in the management and administration of day-to-day operations in branch offices and administrative support units for a large national bank. Major strengths in workflow production, research and problem solving, heavy customer service inter-action, staffing and personnel administration, IRA and 401K administration, and general ledger accounting. A dependable, thorough and well organized planner with a successful track record in loss prevention, customer satisfaction and retention, increasing personnel morale and production, and technical expertise in audit and compliance regulations.

ACCOMPLISHMENTS

WORKFLOW PRODUCTION AND PROJECT DIRECTING

- Developed and implemented operating procedures for the Retirement Plans Administration Unit, eliminating over $300,000 in overtime expense annually.
- Headed and administered all aspects of operations for a unit involving disturbances, new accounts, customer service, general accounting, research, and government reporting.
- Implemented and administered an accounting system for the unit, developing personalized general ledger accounts and a specialized cost center in order to identify all assets, liabilities, income and expense.
- Created and developed accounting and control procedures for the collection, remittance, balancing and year end reporting of tax withholding to the federal and state agencies.
- Increased productivity over 50% by formulating and administering the operational and audit criteria for an automated disbursement function and on-line file system.

RESEARCH/PROBLEM SOLVING AND LOSS PREVENTION

- Recovered 2.5MM in potential losses and set up control procedures to avoid re-occurrence.
- Developed and enforced stringent audit procedures for the disbursement on IRA and KEOGH accounts for a $2.5 billion portfolio, thereby eliminating the possibility of losses and fraudulent activity.
- Alerted to unusual activity, uncovered and investigated fraudulent activity involving forgeries, saving the bank over $700,000 in losses.
- Transformed poor audit ratings and exceptions to a consistent "excellent rating" from 1980-1990.

- Researched, investigated, responded and administered all 1991 year-end IRA reporting corrections within a 60-day period (meeting IRS deadlines) from over 650 banking offices - totaling over 950 corrections.
- Researched and responded with extensive supporting documentation to the IRS to dispel a 1987 and 1988 tax lien, saving the bank over $200,000.

CUSTOMER SERVICE

- Reduced the number of accounts requiring special handling by 75% after centralization, through system improvements and customer negotiations.
- Achieved a 90% improvement in teller line "gridlock" by implementing check-cashing procedures.
- Won consistent recognition for banking offices in accelerating quality customer service by resolving customer disputes and discrepancies in an expedient time frame.

TEAMBUILDING

- Initiated monthly staff meetings and employee of the month awards, increasing staff morale, performance and involvement.
- Created and implemented cross-selling techniques to an operations staff that increased banking office sales in loans, payroll, and trust services by 30%.
- Developed and conducted management meetings and seminars for exempt and non-exempt staff in the areas of affirmative action, regulatory requirements, workplace safety, and introduction of all new operational procedures and marketing products.
- Established and communicated expected standards of performance, reviewed actual performance, counseled, career-coached, resulting in a cohesive department that delivered service effectively.

WORK HISTORY

SECURITY PACIFIC NATIONAL BANK   **1977-1995**

VP Operations, Retirement Plans Administration   1990-1995

VP Operations, South Pasadena Office   1988-1990

VP Operations, Wilshire Grand Office   1985-1988

AVP Operations, AVP Loans, Headquarters Office   1980-1985

Assistant Manager, Various Branch Offices   1977-1980

EDUCATION

Pasadena City College, Pasadena, CA: Courses in Business Administration

---

CHRONOLOGICAL/PLANT OPERATIONS: BREWING & BOTTLING

Name
Address
Telephone

SUMMARY

Twenty years of experience in operations/manufacturing management with two Fortune 500 companies. Background includes:

- New Plant Start-Ups
- Empowerment and Team Management
- Diversity Training
- New Product and Package Introduction
- Hazardous Waste Management
- High-Speed Equipment Technology

- Manning Reduction and Cost Improvements
- Union Contract Negotiations/Administration
- World Class Maintenance
- Corporate Quality Standards
- Distributor Relations
- Fixed and Variable Budget Preparation/Administration

EXPERIENCE

BREWMEISTER COMPANY, Los Angeles, CA   **1975 - Present**
Packing Manager   1989 - Present

Responsibilities:

Report to Operations Manager. Responsible for overall department operations, directing activities of 36 salaried employees and 500 operators, with budget responsibility of $100 + million.

Accomplishments:

- On a continuous basis, streamlined operations through improved equipment reliability, operator development, realignment of job duties and reduction in work force resulting in saving of over $11 million over the last three years.
- Instituted Total Quality Management process resulting in record performance in corporate-administered internal compliance audits and a 30% reduction in scrap rates.
- Coordinated new product start-ups. All start-ups showed operational profit ahead of schedule.
- Planned and directed department Career Development Program, resulting in promotions or interdepartmental movement of over 50% of management staff in a three-and-a-half year period.
- Implemented a World Class Maintenance Program resulting in a 15% reduction in maintenance out-of-service time and a 25% reduction in major line changeover times.
- Founding member of the Plant Cultural Diversity Task Team. Administered a $500,000 plant-wide Diversity Educational Program.

- Coordinated efforts resulting in 50% reduction of solid waste to landfill and three-fold increase in revenues from sales of scrap.
- Developed the long-range master plan for the company's Packaging Operations which is projected to reduce costs corporation-wide by $91 million a year by the year 2000.

Distribution Manager   1984 - 1989

Responsibilities:

Responsible for plant production scheduling, material receiving, warehousing, shipping and traffic functions. Responsible for the activities of 24 salaried and 150 union employees.

Accomplishments:

- Installed new computerized distributor order handling system and truck control systems resulting in $600,000 in labor savings per year.
- Phased out all off-site warehouse storage through consolidation and reduction n finished goods inventory. Eliminate $700,000 in annual warehouse rental fees.
- Improved truck-loading efficiency from 11 trucks per person per shift, to 14 per shift through a series of procedural changes.

Brewery Services Manager   1982 - 1984

Responsibilities:

Responsible for combing the previously independent functions of Industrial Engineering, Production Control, Plant Sanitarium, Manpower Coordination and Cost Improvement. Supervised 20 management employees.

Accomplishments:

- Developed and administered $7.5 million in cost improvement capital spread across 60 projects in all departments. Minimum 25% return on investment achieved for all projects.
- Increased plant production capacity by 10% over a two-year period.

Quality Assurance Manager   1980 - 1982

Responsibilities:

Directed the activities of 30 salaried and 25 union laboratory workers. Coordinated the activities of the Microbiology Lab, analytical chemistry functions, packaging line quality monitoring, technical packaging (materials) and sensory evaluation.

Accomplishments:

- Managed the phased shut-down of laboratory functions in an old facility while simultaneously starting up operations in a new $250 million brewery.
- Reduced consumer complaint frequency by half, from the highest among the six plants to second lowest.

Unit Manager, Packing Quality Control	1979 - 1980
Unit Manager, Product Quality Control	1977 - 1979
Quality Control Supervisor/Group Supervisor	1975- -1977

USA BREWING COMPANY, Indianapolis, IN   **1972 - 1975**

Quality Control Manager
Quality Control Microbiologist
Quality Control Technician

EDUCATION AND TRAINING

MELMAN UNIVERSITY, Bachelor of Science

Lauhoff GMP Program
Juran's Management of Quality Seminar
Kaleel Jamison's Managing Cultural Diversity Workshop
Kepner Tregor Problem Solving Seminar
PERSONNEL DECISIONS, INC., Leadership Program

CHRONOLOGICAL/RECEPTIONIST

NAME

ADDRESS   PHONE

SUMMARY

Sixteen years experience in switchboard operation and clerical support. Reliable, honest, and conscientious employee who can work under direct or indirect supervision. Able to complete assigned duties efficiently and enthusiastically.

PROFESSIONAL EXPERIENCE

INTERNATIONAL TRANSPORT, INC. Chicago, IL   **1988 - Present**
Receptionist - Switchboard Operator

Responsibilities:

Operated Horizon switchboard; typed on IBM Selectric II; kept daily records for month-end reports; handled hotel and plane reservations for company officers.

Accomplishments:

- ◆ Maintained excellent job ratings and attendance.
- ◆ Created numerous master formats, resulting in enhanced ability to track locations of all trucks and railroad cars.
- ◆ Reduced time spent typing by 30% by creation of consolidated forms.
- ◆ Trained other employees in key clerical support functions.
- ◆ Established customer relations.
- ◆ Coordinated social events, including yearly outing with budget of $75,000.

BIG STEEL, INC., Chicago, IL   **1978 - 1988**
Receptionist - Switchboard Operator

Responsibilities:

Operated switchboard; typed purchase orders, invoices, letters, etc.; maintained files and daily records.

Accomplishments:

- ◆ Organized filing systems that resulted in faster retrieval of key information.
- ◆ Established customer relations.

EDUCATION

Courses at Chicago Business College

CHRONOLOGICAL/SALES

Name
Address
Telephone

SUMMARY

Over fifteen years with Fortune 300 company in customer service, expediting, and clerical operations. Conscientious resourceful, and flexible; enjoy being a team worker as well as taking leadership. Excellent skills in communicating key data to employees, customers, and suppliers.

EMPLOYMENT HISTORY

PBG COMPANY, Brookfield and Milwaukee, WI   **1982 - Present**
Sales Assistant   1990 - Present

Responsibilities:

Provided all sales support for 25 field offices and 95 sales representatives. Maintained all customer service functions for the contractor market.

Accomplishments:

- Created a systematic method for expediting pre- and post-order functions, improving processing time by 20%.

- Provided accurate, detailed telephone information which reduced number of customer calls by 25%.

- Maintained order entry, change orders, order shipment tracers, while keeping customers informed.

- Reduced telephone calls by communicating effectively through fax machine.

- Using IBM PC, kept order status updated and performed billing reconciliation for large contractor orders.

- Negotiated product returns, resolved billing and shipping errors . Helped save several key accounts by resolving these quickly and diplomatically.

NAME

Sales Assistant, PGB Automation Sales Subsidiary   1988 - 1990

Responsible for quoting product and parts and all related customer service functions.

Accomplishments:

- Coordinated with factories, customer and service engineering to resolve on-the-job problems with complex electronics equipment.
- Controlled orders while keeping all significant people informed.
- Enhanced customer relationships by initiating practice of calling all customers once a week.
- Negotiated prices and prepared proposals.

Expediter, Apparatus Distribution Sales Division   1986 - 1988

Responsible for customer service in the construction market.

Accomplishments:

- Developed a master data system to expedite large multi-product construction jobs.
- Coordinated jobs from entry through completion.
- Organized and created a network system for product departments, which improved access to key information.

Clerical Assistant, Customer Service and Distribution Operation   1982 - 1986

Responsible for typing, switchboard, mail, purchasing, internal billing.

Accomplishments:

- Typed large quantities of daily data while learning the industry's terminology.
- Cataloged and maintained all supplies for internal company clients.

TRAINING

Company-Sponsored Training - Project Management, Excellence in Customer Service

Milwaukee Area Technical College - Secretarial Science course work

Juneau High School - Milwaukee, WI - Diploma

CHRONOLOGICAL/SALES: BUSINESS SERVICES

NAME
Address ◆ Telephone

SUMMARY

Over 18 years as a professional with solid sales results, consistently making and exceeding goals. Prospect, qualify and close deals while maintaining a quality customer service relationship. Detail oriented and proficient at follow up and follow through.

ACCOMPLISHMENTS

CREDIT INCORPORATED,   **1980 - Present**

Senior Territory Manager
Responsible for the development and maintenance of an establishment/merchant network in the Los Angeles County market.

- ◆ Expanded territory from Los Angeles to 13 Southern and Central California counties.

- ◆ Finished in the top 30% of the national sales force, annually.

- ◆ Recognized with bonus incentives for signing the most top holdouts in region.

- ◆ Achieved recognition as a repeat winner of President's Club.

- ◆ Increased new customer ability to use service by decreasing processing time 50%. Received special recognition for implementation of suggestion that facilitated use of service.

- ◆ Signed 30 restaurants in one month, exceeding goal by 100%.

- ◆ Increased restaurant coverage from 65% to 76% in territory.

- ◆ Signed top "gold" account for two consecutive years.

- ◆ Signed over 300 restaurants per year.

BUSINESS SYSTEMS INC.   **1978 - 1980**
Sales Representative

Sold business systems to a wide variety of organizations.

EDUCATION

B.F.A., Communication Arts, New York Institute of Technology.

> ## BIOGRAPHICAL PRESENTATION
> ## "BIO"

Alex Green
Graphic Designer

As Lead Designer for Karr Industries, Alex has provided the Marketing and Communications Group with creative design services, developing and implementing project identity programs, newsletters, custom brochures, and related sales/marketing material.

Alex applies expertise in design to a broad range of corporate, institutional and private development applications of communications graphics that most effectively enhance project identity and marketability.

Alex has created marketing materials for numerous mixed-use, office, resort and special facility projects including Gulf & Western's Corporate Headquarters, Marola Conference Center and Katon Mountain Village Ski Resort. Alex also produced custom leasing materials for Cameron Village Shopping Center revitalization in Denver, Colorado and the 800-acre Grand Harbor Retirement Community in Guild Harbor, Florida.

Project identity efforts include facility and food service signage as well as menu graphics for Connecticut General Life Insurance Company, Sarasota Quay Waterfront Center and the Pavilion at Silicon Valley Financial Center in San Jose, California.

Alex is a graduate of the Rhode Island School of Design in Providence, Rhode Island, and is a member of the American Institute of Graphic Arts, the Graphic Artists Association of America and the Art Director's Club.

SAMPLE INTERNET RESUME

JOHN C. QUE

1234 56Th Street, N.E., Suite 986
Columbus, Ohio 40303 USA
Phone or Fax: (612) 987-1234
E-mail: abc@mindwell.com

KEYWORDS

GENERAL MANAGER, OPERATIONS MANAGER, INTERNATIONAL OPERATIONS
MANAGEMENT, STRATEGIC PLANNER, SALES MANAGER, MARKETING MANAGER,
MANAGEMENT CONSULTANT, ACCOUNT DEVELOPER, INTERNATIONAL SALES, SALES
TRAINER, WRITER, PUBLIC SPEAKER

SUMMARY

High-energy executive with 18 years achievement creating and directing successful business
ventures in the United States and internationally. Project specialist able to function effectively both
as consultant and permanent team member, and sales leader with a reputation for handling
difficult clients and large accounts. Analytical professional with the experience to make good
financial and strategic business decisions, and with the courage to implement plans rapidly.
Internet/intranet marketing and communications knowledgeable.

ACCOMPLISHMENTS

Marketing and Sales:

Created a total-enterprise approach to technical sales, focusing on enterprise-level selling to
achieve 60% revenue growth plus 20% profit improvement.

Designed and implemented enterprise-wide account penetration strategies. Activities resulted in
tightening market focus, 140% revenue accomplishment and 22% profit growth.

Developed a strategic business relationship between major clients and outside organizations in the
US and internationally, resulting in $11M orders in a client-funded development arrangement.

Managed total effort to bring new network-based messaging products to the US marketplace,
including concept analysis, sales packaging, and P&L planning. Pioneered an alliance strategy for
product co-development and service bureau deployment, virtually eliminating cost to deploy risk.

Strategic Direction:

Designed and implemented an organizational structure for a new $30M venture to rapidly provide
worldwide product implementation and support. Results were management of an organizationally
imposed two-year hiring deferment while still exceeding growth and profit goals by 70%.

I - 31

Conceived and implemented the re-deployment of a large field sales organization to provide market focus and direction. Results were improved revenues and 27% better profit.

Developed strategic partnerships with IBM and others to deliver management automation systems worldwide, eliminating pass-through costs, reducing prices 16% and reducing deployment risk.

Operations:

Established and managed a successful operation for global deployment, including a first presence in the Americas, Europe and Africa. Results were over plan first year sales of $21M.

Reversed negative financial performance, client management problems and corporate image in North America. Efforts provided successful account position and $20M revenue recovery.

Consolidated and managed a technical service/support business, resulting in 215% revenue growth and 42% profit enhancement with existing and new large account penetration.

PROFESSIONAL EXPERIENCE

EVERYWHERE CONSULTING, Columbus, Ohio 1994 - Present

Owner, Management Consultant, Business Developer

Providing temporary organizational development and management expertise in support of manufacturing, software, service and marketing corporations... including sales force development, product development, senior staff development and turnaround implementation. Specialized consultation focusing on technical services consolidation and cost reduction are also provided.

XYZ AUTOMATION, INC., Cincinnati, Ohio 1989 - 1994

Operations Manager, Enterprise Management Systems Division (1992 - 1994)

Developed and managed all aspects of marketing, installation and support for a new manufacturing management and decision support software product suite. Provided world-wide strategic marketing and business development leadership, and delivering far above expectations on three continents.

Regional Manager, Atlanta, Georgia, Process Automation Services (1989 - 1992)

Planned and implemented operations, P&L, sales and staff for a technical field services business. Focused on customers, contract performance, warranty (cost) management and product development, and achieved over 110% growth each year in this business turnaround role.

YOUR FAVORITE CORPORATION, Philadelphia, Pennsylvania 1978 - 1989

Branch Manager, Orlando, Florida (1987 - 1989)

Provided P&L, operations and sales leadership for a new business. Developed new products and methods targeted for deployment on an enterprise-wide basis and tripled revenues during tenure.

National Market Manager, Philadelphia, Pennsylvania (1985 - 1987)

Managed sales, marketing and strategic planning, and growing this business at a 60% rate to $45M.

National Sales Specialist, Montgomery, Alabama (Based) (1978 - 1982) National Account Manager, Montgomery, Alabama (Based) (1982 - 1985)

Contributed 400% of plan first year, with average 230% annual base increases thereafter, and then managed corporate level multi-site account activity, resulting in 187% growth 1983-1985.

EDUCATION

Bachelor of Arts, University of Hometown Graduate Studies: Business Administration and Computer Science

Specialized training in: P & L Enhancement, Human Resource Utilization, Behavioral Interviewing, Management Development & Effectiveness and Team Development

Internet capable with proficiency in a broad variety of business and technical computing functions

ORGANIZATIONS

Client-Associate - Steven-Jane, Inc. (International Sales and Account Management)

Widget Development & Management Association (PDA)

Business Mentor - University of Hometown, School of Business, MBA Program (Entrepreneurial)

Name
Address
Phone

SUMMARY OF QUALIFICATIONS

Senior sales and marketing professional with a solid record of achievement in multiple product lines. Developed and implemented strategic plans driving market development, new product launches, advertising, promotional programming, sales growth and profitability. Expertise in all channels of distribution.

PROFESSIONAL EXPERIENCE

Homelife Building Products Co., Columbus, Ohio, 1994-Present
Director of Retail Sales

- Assumed management responsibility for the sales, marketing and profitability of product generating $72,000,000+ in sales to Homelife National Accounts.
- Directed sales and marketing effort resulting in a 15% sales increase for Homelife Retail Sales in 1995.

Porridge Industries, Inc., Fairfax, Ohio, 1993-1994
National Accounts Sales Manager

- Developed company's National Account strategy, objectives, and programming providing a means of selling major accounts on a direct basis of sale without alienating existing distributor network.
- Sold Your Home's mid-west region Porridge line of doors establishing incremental business generating $1,500,000 in 1994.

Dogwood Flooring, Nashville, Tennessee, 1990-1993
Director of Marketing

- Developed nationwide Key Account program to focus and leverage company resources, resulting in sales increases in excess of 50% with participants.
- Introduced new product family to spearhead growth in underdeveloped market segment. In two years, products grew to represent over 10% of company sales.

Hardy Flooring Division, International WellBilt Inc., 1986-1990
Henryville, New Jersey
Marketing Manager

- Initiated and directed complete updating of division's image to one that projected industry leadership and merchandising superiority over competition.
- Successfully launched new luxury product line, providing entry into high-end residential market segment.

Congeleum Corporation, Kittery, New Jersey, 1979-1986
Director of Mass Merchandiser Products, 1985-1986

- Managed products generating $48,000,000 in sales.
- Established policies, procedures, pricing strategies and guidelines to govern and target company efforts.

Director of Advertising and Public Relations, 1983-1985

- Controlled $12,000,000 - $15,000,000 Advertising and Public Relations budget.
- Directed efforts of five outside agencies in the development and execution of all Advertising and Public Relations activities.

Director of Marketing Services, 1981-1983

- Directed creative effort, procurement and production necessary to launch all promotions, merchandising programs and products.
- Instituted budgetary systems resulting in saving of 5% of $10,000,000 budget during first year of responsibilities.

Merchandising Services Manager, 1979-1981

- Procured and maintained inventory of merchandising support materials averaging $1,000,000 in value.
- Managed the creation and launch of new Do-it-Yourself merchandising program, providing a vehicle for successful market expansion drive.

Worldstrong Industries, Harrisburg, Pennsylvania, 1972-1979
Supervisor, Corporate Merchandising Services, 1977-1979

- Developed promotions and merchandising strategies supporting products from three divisions to National Accounts.

Marketing Representative, Building Materials, 1972-1977

- Led New England in sales performance against budget in Rochester, NY market.
- Increased sales volume by 40% during three years in Montgomery, AL market.

EDUCATION

MBA, University of Bridgeport, Bridgeport, Connecticut
BA, Franklin & Marshall College, Lancaster, Pennsylvania

EMPLOYMENT APPLICATION FORM

Application for Employment

(Please Print)

XYZ, Inc. considers applicants for all positions without regard to race, color, religion, sex, national origin, age, veteran status, or non-job related disability.

Date: _June 5, 1992_

Name: _Johnson_ _Christine_

      last   first   middle

Address: _23 Any Road_ _Chicago_ _IL_ _11111_

       city   state   zip code

Phone: _(312) 555-1111_   Social Security number: _123-45-6789_

     area code

Position(s) applied for: _Switchboard Operator, Administrative or Clerical support_

Available to work:
- (xx) Full-time
- (xx) Days
- (xx) Part-time
- (xx) Evenings

Referral source:
- ( ) Advertisement
- (xx) Friend
- ( ) Employment agency
- ( ) Relative
- ( ) Other

Have you ever been employed by XYZ, Inc. before? ( ) Yes (xx) No Date: _____

Do you have any relatives already employed by XYZ, Inc.? (xx) Yes ( ) No

     If yes, please list names: _Linda Smith, aunt_

Are you above the minimum working age of 18? (xx) Yes ( ) No

Are you a U.S. citizen? (xx) Yes ( ) No

     If no, do you possess an alien registration card? ( ) Yes ( ) No

     If yes, please provide your alien registration number: _____

Have you ever been convicted of a felony? ( ) Yes (xx) No

     If yes, please explain: _____

Have you served in the U.S. Military services? ( ) Yes (xx) No Branch? _____

     Briefly describe your duties: _____

EDUCATION AND TRAINING

Type of School	Name and Location	Dates Attended	Honors Received Diploma/Degree	Course of Study
Elementary School	Toddville School Chicago, IL	1964-1970		
Junior High/ High School	Lakeland Jr. HS Lakeland HS Chicago, IL	1970-1972 1972-1976	Diploma	Business curriculum
College/ University				
Trade/Technical School	Chicago Business College Chicago, IL	1991 - present	Working toward Certificate in Office Practices	Business/ Office Practices

I - 36

References

Present/Former employers:

	Name	Address	Phone
1.	Rev. Thomas Smith, United Church, 2 Holy Way, Chicago, IL (312) 555-3333		
2.	Ms. Susan Jones, Esq., Hutchins, Crutchins and Jones, Attys., 3 Litigation Circle, Chicago, IL (312) 555-4444		
3.	Prof. Donald Wade, Chicago Business College, 4 Education Sq., Chicago, IL (312) 555.-5555		

Employment Experience

Please list present or most recent employer first. If additional space is needed, continue on a separate sheet of paper.

Employer: International Transport, Inc.   Phone: (312) 555-1111
                                                      area code

Address: 42 Railroad Way, Chicago, IL 11111
               street   city   state   zip code

Position(s): Receptionist/Switchboard Operator   Supervisor/Mgr.: Jane Margolis

Dates employed: From: _____ To: _____   Starting $: will discuss   Ending $ will discuss

Reason for leaving: Company relocating out of state and closing facility

Description of primary responsibilities: Operated Horizon switchboard; clerical/administ. duties using IBM Selectric II, kept daily records compiled into month end reports; made hotel and plane reservations for company executives

Employer: Big Steel, Inc.   Phone: (312) 555-0000
                                           area code

Address: 92 Iron Highway, Chicagl, IL 11111
               street   city   state   zip code

Position(s): Receptionist/Switchboard   Supervisor/Mgr.: Al Cirelli

Dates employed: From: _____ To: _____   Starting $: will discuss   Ending $: will discuss

Reason for leaving: Found better position

Description of primary responsibilities: Operated switchboard, typed purchsae orders, invoices, and letters maintained files and daily records.

Employer: _____   Phone: _____
                                                      area code

Address: _____
               street   city   state   zip code

Position(s): _____   Supervisor/Mgr.: _____

Dates employed: From: _____ To: _____   Starting $: _____   Ending $: _____

Reason for leaving: _____

Description of primary responsibilities: _____

I understand that false or misleading information may result in termination of employment.
I authorize XYZ, Inc. to conduct a reference check so that a hiring decision may be made. In the event that XYZ, Inc. is unable to verify any references stated on this application, it is my responsibility to furnish the necessary documentation.
(xx) You may   ( ) You may not contact my present employer
(xx) You may   ( ) You may not contact the schools I have attended for the release of my education records

If accepted for employment with XYZ, Inc., I agree to abide by all of its policies and procedures.
I also agree to have my photograph taken for identification purposes if hired.

Signed: _____   Date: _____

EMPLOYMENT APPLICATION FORM

Application for Employment
(Please Print)

XYZ, Inc. considers applicants for all positions without regard to race, color, religion, sex, national origin, age, veteran status, or non-job related disability.

Date: _____

Name: _____
        last   first   middle

Address: _____
        city   state   zip code

Phone: _____ Social Security number: _____
    area code

Position(s) applied for: _____

Available to work: ( ) Full-time   ( ) Part-time
                       ( ) Days   ( ) Evenings

Referral source: ( ) Advertisement   ( ) Employment agency
                       ( ) Friend   ( ) Relative ( ) Other

Have you ever been employed by XYZ, Inc. before? ( ) Yes ( ) No Date: _____

Do you have any relatives already employed by XYZ, Inc.? ( ) Yes ( ) No
    If yes, please list names: _____

Are you above the minimum working age of 18? ( ) Yes ( ) No

Are you a U.S. citizen? ( ) Yes ( ) No
    If no, do you possess an alien registration card? ( ) Yes ( ) No
    If yes, please provide your alien registration number: _____

Have you ever been convicted of a felony? ( ) Yes ( ) No
    If yes, please explain: _____

Have you served in the U.S. Military services? ( ) Yes ( ) No Branch? _____
    Briefly describe your duties: _____

EDUCATION AND TRAINING

Type of School	Name and Location	Dates Attended	Honors Received Diploma/Degree	Course of Study
Elementary School				
Junior High/ High School				
College/ University				
Trade/Technical School				

References

Present/Former employers:

	Name	Address	Phone
1.			
2.			
3.			

Employment Experience

Please list present or most recent employer first. If additional space is needed, continue on a separate sheet of paper.

Employer: _____ Phone: _____
area code

Address: _____
street   city   state   zip code

Position(s): _____ Supervisor/Mgr.: _____

Dates employed: From: _____ To: _____ Starting $: _____ Ending $ _____

Reason for leaving: _____

Description of primary responsibilities: _____
_____

Employer: _____ Phone: _____
area code

Address: _____
street   city   state   zip code

Position(s): _____ Supervisor/Mgr.: _____

Dates employed: From: _____ To: _____ Starting $: _____ Ending $: _____

Reason for leaving: _____

Description of primary responsibilities: _____
_____

Employer: _____ Phone: _____
area code

Address: _____
street   city   state   zip code

Position(s): _____ Supervisor/Mgr.: _____

Dates employed: From: _____ To: _____ Starting $: _____ Ending $: _____

Reason for leaving: _____

Description of primary responsibilities: _____
_____

I understand that false or misleading information may result in termination of employment.
I authorize XYZ, Inc. to conduct a reference check so that a hiring decision may be made. In the event that XYZ, Inc. is unable to verify any references stated on this application, it is my responsibility to furnish the necessary documentation.
(xx) You may   ( ) You may not contact my present employer
(xx) You may   ( ) You may not contact the schools I have attended for the release of my education records

If accepted for employment with XYZ, Inc., I agree to abide by all of its policies and procedures.
I also agree to have my photograph taken for identification purposes if hired.

Signed: _____ Date: _____

DATA SHEET - CHRISTINE JOHNSON

Social Security #   123-45-6789

EDUCATION

Elementary School - Toddville School, Chicago, IL

Attended 9/64 - 6/70

Junior High School - Lakeland Junior High School, Chicago, IL   Attended 9/70 - 6/72

High School - Lakeland Senior High School, Chicago, IL
   Attended 9/72 - 6/76
   Course of Study: Pre-Business
   Activities: Secretary of Business Club

Courses at Chicago Business College, Office Practices   1993 - present
Certificate Program

FORMER EMPLOYERS

Employer:	International Transport, Inc.
Address:	42 Railroad Way, Chicago, IL
Phone:	(312) 555-1111
Dates employed:	June 1988 - Present
Position(s):	Receptionist/Switchboard Operator
Supervisor:	Jane Margolis
Reason for leaving:	Company is moving the operation to Calitfornia and closing local facility
Primary responsibilities:	(see resume)
Beginning salary:	$15,000/yr.
Ending salary:	$22,500/year

Employer:	Big Steel, Inc.
Address:	92 Iron Highway, Chicago, IL
Phone:	(312) 555-0000
Dates employed:	August 1978 - June 1988
Position(s):	Receptionist/Switchboard
Supervisor:	Al Cirelli
Reason for leaving:	Found better position
Primary responsibilities:	(see resume)
Beginning salary:	$12,000/yr.
Ending salary:	$14,000/year

PERSONAL REFERENCES

Rev. Tom Smith
United Church
2 Holy Way, Chicago, IL 11111
Home (312) 111-1111
Work (312) 222-2222

Ms. Susan Jones, Esq.
Hutchins, Crutchins and Jones, Attorneys,
3 Litigation Circle,
Chicago, IL 11111
Home (312) 333-3333
Work (312) 444-4444

Prof. Donald Wade
Chicago Business College
4 Education Square, Chicago, IL 11111
Home (312) 550-1111
Work (312) 550-2222

II.
Research & Targeting
CUSTOMER-ASSESSMENT

Table of Contents

I. BUSINESS REFERENCES AND DIRECTORIES

Business references and directories will be useful to you in planning your work search strategy. Those listed below can be found at your local business, public college and university libraries. In addition, local directories published by the Chamber of Commerce and government agencies are available in many urban areas. You are encouraged to use all available research sources.

The most efficient way to locate the information you are seeking is to begin with the Preface and Table of Contents of any reference book you are using.

The reference materials below are grouped in reverse order of specialization -- from listings that contain general directory information to more specific listings. With that in mind, you can start with the references that are most appropriate for finding the information you need. Specifically:

A.   Guides to Directories, Associations and Publications

B.   Corporate Ownership Ties

C.   Organizations and Their Executives

D.   Organizations by Specific Category

E.   Management and Officers' Profiles

F.   Middle Management Positions

I-A. GUIDES TO DIRECTORIES, ASSOCIATIONS AND PUBLICATIONS

Guide to American Directories

B. Klein Publications, P.O. Box 8503, Coral Springs, FL 33065.

- A listing and description of 6,000 directories with over 300 major industrial, professional and mercantile classifications.

The Directory of Directories (2 vols.)

Gale Research Group, Book Tower, Detroit, MI 48226.

- 10,400 listings in three sections -- directory, title and keyword index, and subject index.
- Useful in locating membership names and titles.

Encyclopedia of Associations (2 vols.)

Gale Research Co., Book Tower, Detroit, MI 48226.

- A guide to 22,000 national nonprofit organizations of all types and interests including commodity exchanges; public administration; military, cultural, patriotic, and scientific organizations; fraternities; sororities; and fan clubs. Gives contact names, headquarters' addresses, telephone numbers, chief officials, number of members and chapters, descriptions of membership, aims and activities. Includes lists of special committees and departments, publication, and a 4-year convention schedule. Arranged by subject and cross-referenced by name of chief executive and geographic location, as well as by organization name.
- Useful in locating placement committees which can help you learn of specific job openings in your field of interest, getting membership lists of individuals in order to develop personal contacts and learning where and when conferences are being held so that you can attend them.

Business Organizations, Agencies and Publications Directory (2 vols.)

Gale Research Inc., Book Tower, Detroit, MI 48226. (Biannual)

- Lists business names, addresses and contact person of approximately 24,000 organizations and publications that are important and varied sources of data and information on all areas of business, including trade, commercial and labor organizations, government agencies, stock exchange, diplomatic offices and banks, tourism, publishing, computer information services, etc.

Moody's Industry Review

Moody's Investors Service, Inc., Dun and Bradstreet Company, 99 Church Street, New York, NY 10007. (Annual with weekly updates of 11 industries per issue)

- Ranks 4,000 leading companies in 145 industry categories according to standard financial criteria: revenues, price-earnings ratio, net income, profit margin and return on capital. Classified by industry. Arranged by company name.

U.S. Industrial Directory

A Reed International Publication. (Annual)

- Four volumes provide over 50,000 company names, addresses, trade names and phone numbers of industrial entries, as well as addresses and phone numbers of local sales offices and distributors.

Directory of Industry Data Resources (5 vols.)

Ballinger Publishing Company, Harper & Row Publishers, Inc., 54 South Church Street, Cambridge, MA 02138.

- Lists 3,000 publishers of industry data sources including bibliographic and source data bases, indexing and abstracting services, and market research firm. Describes monographs, surveys, periodical special issues, market studies, etc., covering 65 industries. Lists company names, address and phone. Arranged alphabetically and by type of publication service.

- Three volumes cover the United States and Canada. Two volumes cover Europe.

National Trade and Professional Associations of the U.S.

Columbia Books, Inc., 1350 New York Avenue, N.W., Suite 207, Washington, D.C. 20005. (Annual in January)

- Lists over 6,000 entries including name, year established, name of chief executive, address, phone number of staff members, budget, size of membership, publications and historical and descriptive data. Also includes date, expected attendance and location of annual meeting. Arranged alphabetically and by location, subject, budget and acronym.

Directory of U.S. Labor Organizations

BNA Books, Bureau of National Affairs, Inc., 1231 25th Street, N.W., Washington, D.C. 20037. (Biennial, fall of even years)

- Lists over 200 national unions, professional and state employee associations engaged in labor representation. Includes name, address, names of elected officials and department heads, publications, conventions, membership figures, number of locals.

- Separate sections for AFL-CIO, railroad unions, other federations, and for individual national unions. Arranged alphabetically by personal name.

Consultants and Consulting Organizations Directory

Gale Research Inc., Book Tower, Detroit, MI 48226.

- Lists more than 14,000 consulting organizations and consultants in two volumes.

- Arranged by industry, by consulting functional category, by geographic location, by personal name and by consulting firm.

- Includes name, address, telephone, principal executives, staff size, purpose and activity.

Directory of Consultants

National Association of Regulatory Utility Commissioners, Box 684, Washington, D.C. 20044. (Annual in December)

- Lists consultants and consulting firms active in utility and transportation industries. Includes firm or individual name, address, and phone; names of regulatory agencies engaged in the past; purpose and dates of past engagements; areas of specialization; qualifications and experience. Arranged alphabetically.

The Career Guide: Dun's Employment Opportunities Directory

Dun's Marketing Services, Dun & Bradstreet Corp., 49 Old Bloomfield Road, Mountain Lakes, NJ 07046. (Annual in November)

- Lists more than 5,000 companies that have 1,000 or more employees and that may provide career opportunities in sales, marketing, management, engineering, life and physical sciences, computer science, mathematics, statistics planning, accounting and finance, liberal arts fields, and other technical and professional areas. Also covers personnel consultants throughout the country. Includes some public sector employers (e.g., governments, schools) not found in similar lists. Based on data supplied by questionnaire and personal interview.

- Entries include company name, location of headquarters, other offices and plants. May also include name, title, address and phone number of employment contact; disciplines or occupational groups hired; brief overview of company; types of positions that may be available; training and career development programs and benefits offered.

- Companies are arranged alphabetically; consultants are geographical.

Directory of Jobs and Careers Abroad

Vacation-Work, 9 Park End Street, Oxford OX1 1HJ, England. (Triennial)

- Principal content is information on how to seek work abroad.

- Lists agencies, consultants, associations, government agencies, overseas branches, affiliates and subsidiaries of British companies and other organizations which offer or assist in locating permanent jobs abroad. Coverage is worldwide. Entries include organization name, address, phone, name of contact, geographical and career areas covered.

- Arranged by type of career, then geographical.

Dun's Directory of Service Companies

Dun's Marketing Services, Inc., 3 Sylvan Way, Parsippany, NJ 07054.

- Lists 50,000 largest service enterprises nationwide including both public and private companies.

II - 5

Corporate Technology Directory

Corporate Tech. Information Services, Inc., 1 Market Street, P.O. Box 81281, Wellesley Hills, MA 02181-0003.

- Comprehensive reference of over 25,000 U.S. entities that manufacture or develop high technology products. Indexed by name, location, parent name and product.

The Directory of Executive Recruiters

Kennedy & Kennedy, Inc., Templeton Road, Fitzwilliam, NH 03447. (Annual)

- Lists over 2,000 executive recruiter firms.
- Arranged by contingency categories of search; also by function, by industry, by geographic location.
- Includes firm name, principals of firm, address, salary level and key contact.

I-B. CORPORATE OWNERSHIP TIES

Directory of Corporate Affiliations

National Register Publishing Co., Inc., MacMillan Inc., 3004 Glenview Road, Wilmette, IL 60091. (Annual)

- Provides detailed information on "who owns whom" as a result of mergers and acquisitions. Contained are companies listed on the New York Stock Exchange, the American Stock Exchange, the "Fortune 500" and others. Total listing of 4,000 parent companies and 40,000 U.S. affiliates.

- This directory is useful when one is seeking out the detailed corporate structure of a parent company, or when a company is not listed in other directories because it is a subsidiary division or affiliate.

America's Corporate Families: Billion Dollar Directory (2 vols.)

Dun's Marketing Services, Inc., 3 Sylvan Way, Parsippany, NJ 07054.

- Identifies over 8,000 major U.S. parent companies and their subsidiaries and divisions (over 44,000). To be listed, companies must conduct business in at least two locations with controlling interest in at least one subsidiary, and have a net worth of at least $500,000.

- Gives DUNS number and state of incorporation for parent companies, as well as directory information for all companies; also lists Standard Industrial Classification (SIC) codes and stock exchange symbols, principal bank, accounting and legal firms.

I-C. ORGANIZATIONS AND THEIR EXECUTIVES

Register of Corporations, Directors, and Executives (3 vols.)

Standard and Poor's, 25 Broadway, New York, NY 10004. (Annual)

- A guide to the business community providing information on public companies of the U.S.

  - Volume I. Corporate Listings
    - Alphabetical directory listing by business name of over 45,000 corporations, including names and titles of officers and directors, Standard Industrial Classification (SIC) codes and annual sales.

  - Volume II. Directors and Executives
    - Biographies of 70,000 individuals serving as officers, directors, trustees, etc., and their principal business affiliations, residence addresses, year and place of birth, and fraternal memberships, if available.

  - Volume III. Indexes
    - Listings are indexed by SIC codes and geography. An obituary section records recent deaths of executive personnel. New executives and companies appearing for the first time are included with brief business biographies.

Standard and Poor's Stock Reports

(Revised weekly)

- The stock reports of 800 companies traded on the American Stock Exchange.

Dun & Bradstreet Million Dollar Directory (5 vols.)

Dun's Marketing Services Inc., 3 Sylvan Way, Parsippany, NJ 07054. (Annual)

- A guide to 160,000 public companies in the U.S. with net worth of half a million or more; includes industrial corporations, bank and trust companies, wholesalers, retailers and domestic subsidiaries of foreign corporations. The 5th volume lists the top 50,000 moneymaking companies.

- Alphabetical listings by business name, including address, telephone number, name and title of officers and directors, SIC code, annual sales, number of employees, some division names of principal and secondary businesses, as well as principal bank, legal and accounting firms.

Polk's Bank Directory

North American Edition. R. L. Polk Company, 2001 Elm Hill Pike, Nashville, TN 37210-3848. (Semiannual)

- A major detailed directory listing banks, other financial institutions and government agencies by address; also includes geographic indexing, names and titles of officers, financial information, names of discontinued banks and maps. Useful for corporations and government agencies.

Who Owns Whom

Dun & Bradstreet Limited, Holmers Farm Way, High Wycombe, Bucks HP12 4UL, England.

- Indicates ownership of subsidiary and associate companies and how they fit into their parent group.

Best's Insurance Reports, Property and Casualty

A.M. Best Co., Ambest Road, Oldwick, NJ 08858. (Annual)

- As well as addresses, this reference gives in-depth analyses, operating statistics, financial data and ratings, and names of officers in over 1,300 major stock and mutual property-casualty insurance companies. In addition, provides summary data on over 2,000 smaller mutual companies and on 300 casualty companies operating in Canada.

Best's Insurance Reports, Life and Health

A.M. Best Co., Ambest Road, Oldwick, NJ 08858. (Annual)

- Supplies 1,800 individual company reports in addition to summaries of 600 smaller companies in the property and casualty industry.

Securities Dealers of North America

Standard and Poor's, 25 Broadway, New York, NY 10004. (Semiannual with supplements published every 6 weeks)

Lists over 15,000 security dealers alphabetically and by geographic region. Gives names, titles and addresses of company officers; employer's I.D. number and clearing facilities.

Thomas Register of American Manufacturers (21 vols.)

Thomas Publishing Co., One Penn Plaza, New York, NY 10019. (Annual)

■ Lists more than 140,000 specific product manufacturers, both large and small including names of officers, capital assets and parent or subsidiary company.

- Volumes 1 - 11. Lists firms under their product headings (approx. 48,000 products).
- Volume 12. Index to products and services.
- Volume 13. Company profiles.
- Volume 14. Index to the manufacturers by their trade brand names.
- Volumes 15 - 21. Bound catalogues of more than 1,400 of the manufacturing firms.

Corporate Technology Directory (4 vols.)

Corporate Technology Information Services, Inc., One Market Street, Wellesley Hills, MA 02181. (Annual)

■ Contains more than 25,000 corporate profiles indexed by name, product, geography and parent company. All companies listed manufacture/develop high tech products; these volumes give general listing data, including names of key personnel, sales and average revenues.

Directory of American Firms Operating in Foreign Countries (3 vols.)

World Trade Academy Press, 50 E. 42nd Street, New York, NY 10017. (Updated irregularly)

■ Directory listings of approximately 3,000 American corporations with factories and branch offices in 36 countries; names of key contact personnel are given.

Directory of Foreign Firms Operating in the U.S

■ 1600 Foreign firms in 54 countries and nearly 2,700 businesses in the U.S. which they own wholly or in part.

Principal International Businesses (1 vol.)

Dun's Marketing Services Inc., 899 Eaton Avenue, Bethlehem, PA 18025. (Annual)

- Lists nearly 50,000 prominent companies in 133 countries. Grouped by geographic location, product and alphabetically. Text is simultaneously translated into French, Spanish and German (as well as English).

I-D. ORGANIZATIONS BY SPECIFIC CATEGORY

Standard Directory of Advertisers

National Register Publishing Co., Inc., Wilmette, IL 60091. (Annual, with supplements published 5 times yearly)

- Lists 24,000 companies placing national and regional advertising including their names, telephone numbers, products advertised with brand/trade names, the names of 80,000 executives and their titles, as well as the advertising agency handling the account, account executives, media used, distribution.

- Published in two editions; in one volume, companies are listed by product classification or service; in the second volume, companies are grouped according to geographic location.

- A useful tool in locating marketing officers, names of parent companies, subsidiaries and affiliates.

Standard Directory of Advertising Agencies

National Register Publishing Co., Inc., Wilmette, IL 60091. (Published 3 times yearly, monthly supplements)

- Lists a total of 4,400 U.S. and foreign agency establishments including special market index and media services.

Special Market Index

- The view-at-a-glance of agencies specializing in the fields of finance, medicine, resort and travel, African-American and Hispanic markets, media service organizations and sales promotion agencies.

Media Services

- Listing of sales promotion agencies, media services and time-buying organizations.

- Alphabetical listing of advertising agencies, including branches, personnel and accounts. Listing of largest agencies (ranked by annual billings).

- Geographical index of advertising agencies listing names, addresses and telephone numbers of agencies by state and city.

Pratt's Guide to Venture Capital Sources

Venture Economics, Inc., 16 Laurel Ave., Wellesley Hills, MA 02181. (Annual)

■ Directory listings of over 700 (mainly U.S.) venture capital firms, corporate venture groups and small investment corporations. The listings include the investment and industry preferences of each firm.

■ Articles on investment and other related topics are included.

O'Dwyer's Directory of Public Relations Firms

J.R. O'Dwyer Co., Inc., 271 Madison Ave., New York, NY 10016.

■ Directory entries of over 1,900 U.S. and Canadian public relations firms, listed alphabetically, including their overseas offices, clients and billings. Indexed by firm specialty, client and geography; includes a list of the top 50 public relations firms.

I-E. MANAGEMENT AND OFFICERS' PROFILES

Reference Book of Corporate Managements (4 vols.)

Dun & Bradstreet Corporation, 899 Eaton Avenue, Bethlehem, PA 18025. (Annual)

- Contains data on nearly 200,000 presidents, officers and managers of 12,000 credit, personnel and data processing companies. Information includes dates of birth, education and business positions presently and previously held; for directors who are not officers, their present principal business connections are supplied.

- Gives details of corporate officers which are not available in other directories. It also gives the reader some idea of the personality of a corporation by providing information on the technical background of its officers.

I-F. MIDDLE MANAGEMENT POSITIONS

Middle Management Reports (2 vols.)

E.C.S. Wyatt Data Services. (Annual)

■   These volumes contain information contributed by over 1,800 businesses on middle management positions within 17 industries. Information includes ECS industrial classification guide; budget, merit and general increase tables; salary structures; position descriptions; and a table of general wage information grouped by job title.

II. BUREAU OF LABOR STATISTICS PUBLICATIONS

The Bureau of Labor Statistics (BLS) publishes a comprehensive line of bulletins and periodicals devoted to analyzing statistical information that relates to the major occupational fields. Past employment figures and projections by major sector, selected industry and broad occupational group are available to you, as are other published establishment data covering the broad spectrum of economic topics. Salary surveys are also available by industry, by level within an industry and by geographic location.

The Bureau's publications include a number of comprehensive guides to job titles/descriptions within specific areas (e.g., health services and environmental protection), as well as more general references (i.e., the Dictionary of Occupational Titles). These volumes are updated as necessary, as are all the materials containing dated information. Many of the BLS publications are carried by public and college libraries.

The "BLS Update," a quarterly newsletter, is available by subscription. It can be a very valuable publication for your research as it lists updated titles and availability dates of new publications, all of which can be mail-ordered, as well as brief content summaries. Many of the publications are free; others are for sale for a nominal price. The "Update" also contains brief articles and current statistical information covering all areas of the economic scene.

The recorded summaries of statistical data that BLS tapes for telephone hotlines across the country may also be useful in your research. A Bureau economist is available for any questions at one of the hotline numbers. You can obtain the telephone numbers for your area by calling your nearest Bureau/Library of Labor Statistics. These numbers are also published in the "BLS Update."

Some of the data series are available on BLS Data Diskettes. The disks contain the specified data series, as well as the customary uses, if any, for the statistics. You will need an IBM-compatible PC and Lotus 1-2-3 Version 1A or Version 2 if you plan to use the diskettes.

These sources will be valuable to you whether you are considering a career in a new and expanding industry; one within a stable, established field; or if you have yet to decide on the direction of your new career.

A complete catalogue and information on ordering BLS publications is available from:

Bureau of Labor Statistics, Inquiries & Correspondence
441 "G" Street, N.W., Washington, DC 20212

Titles of their publications are listed below.

- Geographic Profiles of Employment, Unemployment
- US Dept. of Labor Statistics Employment, Earnings
- Dictionary of Occupational Titles
- Guide for Occupational Exploration
- Exploring Careers
- Occupational Outlook Handbook
- Projections 2000
- "Monthly Labor Review"
- BLS Update

III. Specific Company Publications

A company's annual report will be useful in identifying the certified public accountant's exceptions "to generally accepted accounting principles," and alerting you to matters that may be crucial to your joining the firm. In addition to the balance sheet and the auditor's report, the annual report also contains a letter from the chairman reflecting the personality, well-being and direction of the company.

This information can be obtained by calling the Investor Relations or Communications departments of the targeted firm and requesting a copy.

There are a limited number of annual reports accessible on the Internet. You can access available company records through the company web page (e.g., www.DBM.com, www.Ford.com, etc.). If the name of the target company does not appear on the company web page, you may also employ other search engines by clicking on "Net Search." Key in the name of the target company and begin the search.

IV. ADDITIONAL PUBLICATIONS AND PERIODICALS

In addition to the preceding, there are numerous industry, Chamber of Commerce and Fortune 500 directories, trade journals and papers. These may be found at your local business, college or university libraries.

- Business Periodical Index
- Directory of Directors
- Directories in Print
- Congressional Directory
- Federal Directory
- Federal Yellow Book
- The College Placement Annual
- Readers' Guide to Periodical Literature
- Encyclopedia of Careers and Vocational Guidance
- Taylor's Encyclopedia of Government Officials
- Directory of American Firms Operating in Foreign Countries

Periodicals

- Barron's
- Business Week
- Business World
- Buyouts and Acquisitions
- Forbes
- Fortune
- Money
- Nation's Business

V. ELECTRONIC DATABASES

OneSource.com

Provides a comprehensive analysis resource that offers immediate access to critical financial and textual information on over 150,000 U.S. public and private companies. The database includes **Market Guide** profiles, providing financial information on over 8,300 public companies, and **Ward's Business Directory**, with information on over 140,000 public and private companies and their major divisions and subsidiaries. Also included in the database are news stories and press releases, provided by **Business Custom Wire**, and are updated twice daily. Industry overviews are available for over 400 industries based on primary research, and **Ivestext** analyst reports are provided for over 4,000 public companies ranging 54 industries. Executive biographies are obtained from both **Marquis Who's Who**, and the **Standard & Poor's Register**, totaling over 100,000 executive biographies. Full text SEC documents are also available. OneSource.com is available on the Internet (http://www.onesource.com).

Dow Vision Live Newsfeeds

This database contains live newsfeeds from news sources to which DBM subscribes in the United States. The information remains in the database for 30 days. Each news source contained in the database is described below.

- *The Wall Street Journal*: Full-text version of articles from *The Wall Street Journal*.

- *Dow Jones News Service*: Real-time stories on over 9,000 companies in the U.S. and world-wide, U.S. government agencies, financial markets and the U.S. economy.

- *Dow Jones International News*: Includes economic reports for comprehensive coverage of economic and political news; the European Corporate Report, for real-time news plus commentary on European companies and stocks; the World Equities Report, for coverage of corporate and equities market news; the International Petroleum Report, for the latest on international oil prices and availability; the Foreign Exchange Report, for providing coverage on foreign exchange rates and news that affects the market; and Bankers Report, for coverage of international money and capital markets.

- Federal Filings: Real-time reports on the latest activity and rulings from the SEC. Provides notices and analysis of significant SEC filings and bankruptcies, as well as mergers and acquisitions activity. Includes disclosures from major shareholders and company insiders, annual and quarterly reports (10Ks and 10Qs), and significant corporate events (8Ks).

- Investext Abstracts: Abstracts of reports on 15,000 companies and industries from the world's leading investment banks and financial research firms.

- Press Release Wires (*PR Newswire* and *Business Wire*): These wires allow you to monitor the latest press announcements for information on U.S. companies. Provided are unedited press releases from businesses, government agencies, industry associations, labor unions and stock exchanges.

- *Japan Economic Newswire*: Same-day, English-language coverage of Japanese business, economic, political and financial news.

- *Capital Markets Report*: Provides up-to-the-second coverage of U.S. and international government securities markets; U.S. agency, corporate and municipal bond activity; Eurobonds; plus money-market instruments and economic indicators from around the world.

- *Professional Investor Report*: Real-time activity reporting is provided on more than 9,000 stocks traded on the New York and American exchanges, as well as the over-the-counter market.

VI. INFORMATION RESOURCE SPECIALISTS

Drake Beam Morin employs an Information Resource Specialist with a Master of Library Science degree. These librarians conduct searches on powerful databases to satisfy the research needs of DBM Candidates (with individual or follow on services) that go beyond the extensive capabilities of our office resources. Information developed by searches is e-mailed, faxed, provided on diskette, or printed out, based on the Candidate's needs.

DBM is constantly evaluating resources that will be of assistance to DBM Candidates in researching the job market and making critical career decisions.

Resources available through the Information Resource Specialists are described below.

Dun's Business Locator

Contains information on 12.4 million companies, including company name (or tradestyle), street address, city, state, zip code, primary SIC code, DUNS number and location status (headquarters or branch office). Since information is limited to location only, it is used to identify companies within certain areas or to find the various facilities operated by a company.

Dun's Market Identifiers

Offers more than 20 selection options, including location, line of business, SIC codes, number of employees, names and titles of principal executives, and a sales trend summary. Both established and start-up companies can be identified by selecting the year the business was started.

Moody's® International Company Data

Features complete financial information on the top non-U.S.-based corporations in over 100 countries, including Moody's News Reports. Valuable when identifying investment opportunities, tracking financial performance, pinpointing M&A candidates, evaluating credit worthiness and monitoring industry trends. Full unaltered financials on over 13,000 public companies including all NYSE, AMEX, NASDAQ-NMS, NASDAQ and OTC Exchange Corporation, and select regional exchange companies.

NEXIS®

One of the world's most comprehensive full-text libraries of company, trade, industry, international news and financial information utilizing more than 750 sources. Frequent updates of wire services from more than 650 worldwide news bureaus, as well as major national and international newspapers, provide timely information.

OneSource U.S. Private+

This resource is a directory product containing summary information on over 179,000 U.S. public and private companies, subsidiaries and major divisions. This extensive coverage allows for a comprehensive listing of participants in an industry or geographic area. The data is taken from *Ward's Business Directory*, the *Directory of Corporate Affiliations/U.S. Private*, and the PROMT® database. Product coverage includes company name and address, primary and secondary SIC codes, total sales and employment, description of business, parent/subsidiary information and article abstracts, as well as the name of the CEO and up to four additional executives.

PhoneDisc®

A speedy, powerful white pages database that provides company name, address, telephone number, business type (SIC code), and contact name for companies across the U.S. Similar to Dun's Business Locator but with greater cross-reference and indexing capabilities.

Dun & Bradstreet Access

Allows access to Business Information Report, Payment Analysis Report, and Credit Advisory System for over 10 million U.S. public and private companies. Reports include information on the history of the company, payments, finance, public filings, a brief business summary, and payments habits of the firm and of the firm's industry. Upon request, Dun & Bradstreet will conduct an investigation of any company that does not appear in the database.

Career Search

Career Search is a database designed specifically for employment search. Containing over 700,000 public and private organizations, Career Search is an easy-to-use system covering all major industries nationwide. Prospective companies may be found using industry, geographic and profile selectable criteria in any number of combinations. Output is available in a summary list of companies, a detailed report or in one of five export formats. Career Search is most helpful for the Candidate in the initial identification of companies that match a particular industry, geographic area and size.

Career Search is a proactive market research tool designed to identify the specific organizations matching your job search criteria. It does not include officer biographies or financial data. After you have identified companies of potential interest, OneSource™ can be used to produce financials and biographies.

VIII. RESUME/JOB LISTING OPPORTUNITIES VIA THE INTERNET

The following Internet Search Engines offer a wealth of information and assistance to the job hunter. The Internet is the world's largest network available for your use 24 hours a day all at your fingertips *so use it*! You can get assistance writing your resume and then post it to employers at no cost in most cases. You have access to the most current information available both locally as well as across the state, country or even the world. The Search Engines list below were accurate at the time of print.[1]

YAHOO	ALTAVISTA
http://www.yahoo.com/	http://altavista.digital.com/
Yahoo finds all keyword matches, then sorts the results according to relevancy within each specific area. Results are ranked in the following manner: <ul><li>documents matching more of the keywords will have a higher rank</li><li>documents matching words found in the title are ranked higher than those found in the body or URL</li><li>categories matching high in the Yahoo tree hierarchy (general categories) are ranked higher than those lower in the hierarchy</li></ul>	AltaVista claims to access the largest Web index: 31 million pages on 476,000 servers, and four million articles from 14,000 Usenet news groups. AltaVista supports Simple or Advanced searching. Simple Search uses machine intelligence to force some of the features of Advanced Search. Advanced gives the searcher more specific control.
EXCITE	**WEBCRAWLER**
http://www.excite.com/	http://www.webcrawler.com/
Excite claims to be the most comprehensive search tool on the Internet, indexing over 50 million Web pages, 60,000 categorized Web-site reviews, and recent Usenet postings. Its search engine uses ICE (intelligent concept extraction) to learn about word relationships. This enables a kind of cross-referencing.	Webcrawler is an outstanding search engine that includes a catalog of pre-classified subjects (directory services). It implements a feature of further searching based on pre-set search terms from the subject catalog, very much like Excite. Webcrawler touts "natural language searching," so you can enter a search like "highest mountain in the world."

[1]http:/daphne.palomar.edu/TGSEARCH/ (various additional Internet available sites - try keyword phrase "search engines" in YAHOO)

IX. FINDING ANSWERS TO COMMONLY ASKED QUESTIONS

Listed below are the types of questions job seekers usually ask, followed by the sources where answers can be found. The questions fall into these general categories:

- Location
- Industries
- Companies
- Employment Organizations

TOPIC	QUESTIONS	SOURCES
Location	What companies are nearby?	Career Search
		State Industrial Directories
		Dun & Bradstreet Reference Book of Corporate Management
		Regional Development Agencies
		Chambers of Commerce, state and local
		Career Search
		Moody's manuals
		Directory of Corporate Affiliations
		Company annual reports and 10-Ks
		Other sources of company information may be used depending on the types of facilities sought (headquarters vs. manufacturing location).
Industries	What are the high-growth industries?	Career Search
		Value Line Investment Surveys

IX. FINDING ANSWERS TO COMMONLY ASKED QUESTIONS
cont.

TOPIC	QUESTIONS	SOURCES
Industries, cont.	What are the high-growth industries?, cont.	Predicast's forecasts manuals
		Refer to the *Directory of Industry Data Sources* for other sources.
	What are the salary levels in specific industries?	American Compensation Association publications (libraries may not have the American Compensation Association or Management Association Surveys)
		The American Almanac of Jobs and Salaries
		American Management Association Surveys
	Who are the competitors?	Career Search
		Dun & Bradstreet Million Dollar Directory by noting other companies making the same product
		Standard & Poor's Industry Survey
		Business Periodicals Index
		Other sources: industry directories/ buyer's guides (check special issues index)
	What industries use specific types of professionals?	*Encyclopedia of Associations*
		National Trade and Professional Associations of the United States (identify appropriate organizations, obtain membership lists, note companies and/or industries)

IX. FINDING ANSWERS TO COMMONLY ASKED QUESTIONS
cont.

TOPIC	QUESTIONS	SOURCES
Industries, cont.	What industries use specific types of professionals?, cont.	*Directory of U.S. Labor Organizations* (identify associations, obtain names of elected officials and department heads)
		The Career Guide: Dun's Employment Opportunities Directory
		Encyclopedia of Career and Vocational Guidance Occupational Outlook Handbook
		Check the library for other occupational guidebooks.
	What are the products of a company?	Career Search
		OneSource™
		Company annual reports
		Moody's Manuals
		Thomas Register company catalog volumes
		U.S. Industrial Directory
		Thomas Register product volumes
	What companies make certain products?	*Dun & Bradstreeet Million Dollar Directory*
		Standard & Poor's Register of Corporations, Directors, and Executives
		Standard Directory of Advertisers
		These are primary sources; other industry catalogs exist.

IX. FINDING ANSWERS TO COMMONLY ASKED QUESTIONS
cont.

TOPIC	QUESTIONS	SOURCES
Industries, cont.	Can consulting organizations be identified by field?	Career Search
		Consultants and Consulting Organizations Directory and companion directories
		There are also many industry specific directories of consultants; see the *Directory of Directories*.
Companies	What are sources of company reports and analysis?	OneSource™ Investext Reports
		Standard & Poor's Stock Report
		Moody's Investors Fact Sheets
		Value Line Investment Surveys
		Wall Street Transcript
		Some libraries may subscribe to other stock analysis services.

IX. FINDING ANSWERS TO COMMONLY ASKED QUESTIONS

cont.

TOPIC	QUESTIONS	SOURCES
Companies, cont.	What are management's practices with regard to training?	Company annual reports, employee relations, training and development sections
		Membership directories for training organizations (e.g., American Society for Training & Development)
		The Career Guide: Dun's Employment Opportunities Directory
		Peterson's Guides
	Who are key people in the company and what are their backgrounds?	OneSource™ bios
		Dun & Bradstreet Reference Book of Corporate Managements
		Standard & Poor's Register of Corporations, Directors, and Executives
		Who's Who directories
		Corporate proxy statements
	Who are the people in the lines of business?	*Dun & Bradstreet's America's Corporate Families*
		State business directories (generally available in public libraries)
		Company annual reports
		Other directories (refer to the *Directory of Directories* and *Directory of Industry Data Sources* for direction)

IX. FINDING ANSWERS TO COMMONLY ASKED QUESTIONS
cont.

TOPIC	QUESTIONS	SOURCES
Employment	What are the names of employment agencies and/or executive recruiters that specialize in a particular field?	Career Search
		The Directory of Executive Recruiters
		There are other directories produced by state and local associations.
	How does one find out about government employment opportunities?	*The State Administrative Officials*
		Classified by Functions has a section listing state employment offices and their telephone numbers.
		The Internet
		Federal: The U.S. Office of Personnel Management (1900 E. Street NW, Washington, DC) is responsible for nationwide recruiting for Civil Service positions at GS levels 1-15; it maintains a network of federal job information centers in major metropolitan areas; telephone numbers are listed in the white pages under U.S. Government, Office of Personnel Management — the New York City office number is (212) 264-0422.

III.
Written
Communication

Table of Contents

1. SAMPLE CUSTOMIZED LETTERS

[A. *Pre-Networking Letter*]

Name
Address
Phone Number

Date

ADDRESSEE
ADDRESSEE TITLE
COMPANY
ADDRESS

Dear *First Name*:

Your name was given to me by Leslie Lucas, who spoke very highly of you and your company. Leslie felt that your broad experience and knowledge would be of great benefit to me.

Like many other organizations my company, Atlas Inc., has experienced a reorganization and, as a result, has severely cut back its mid-management layer. After much deliberation, I have decided to use this as an opportunity to re-position my career.

While I don't expect that you know of any openings, I would appreciate your insight and comments on ways to move my management skills into areas beyond administrative and operations. This is where Leslie felt you could be helpful to me, particularly in your own field.

I will call you next week to arrange a time for a mutually convenient meeting, and look forward to our conversation.

Sincerely,

[A. Pre-Networking Letter to Fellow Alumni]

Name
Address
Phone Number

Date

Addressee
Addressee Title
Company
Address

Dear *First Name*:

As a fellow graduate of (school name), I am writing to ask for your help.

Having spent 13 years with Southwest Commerce Bank, I am looking for a marketing management position in the banking or financial services industries. I hope you will take a moment to look at my resume and suggest one or two people in your network who would be able to move me along in my search for a new position.

My career in the banking industry includes the position of Marketing Manager in the mortgage lending area, as well as experience in marketing bank products and services to a broad range of commercial consumers.

I am a capable generalist with specific expertise in management, business development and loan administration. I would like to join a medium-sized or small financial institution that would benefit from my background and experience.

Frankly, this is a bit of an experiment on my part -- contacting college alumni who would be willing to provide useful suggestions for my search. I hope you would be willing to offer names of other colleagues or financial institutions I could contact, or executive search professionals with whom you have a relationship who would spend a few minutes talking with me.

I would appreciate hearing your suggestions, as well as the opportunity to return the favor in the future. I will call you in a few days, and look forward to speaking with you.

Sincerely,

Enclosure: resume

[B. *Target Marketing Letter*]

Name
Address
Phone Number

Date

Addressee
Addressee Title
Company
Address

Dear *Mr./Ms. Addressee* (or *First Name*, if appropriate):

My research into Sycamore Industries has prompted me to contact you, particularly in light of the fact that I am considering new career alternatives.

I have been impressed with the growth of Sycamore Industries, and know that it is in large part due to your vision of a customer-driven quality effort that has been embraced by other industry leaders. Noting a recent article in Crain's, I could see how the results I produced at National Foods could be an asset to your continuous improvment.

As Customer Service Manager at National Foods, I was instrumental in increasing the quality of customer care, as reported in our most recent customer survey (copy enclosed).

As you can see by the attached resume, my achievements over past four years have improved business. I feel certain I could make a significant contribution to Sycamore's growth, new business acquisition and cost reduction efforts.

I will call your office within the week to see if we can schedule a mutually convenient meeting time to discuss this possibility.

Sincerely,

Enclosure: customer survey

              resume

[B. Target Marketing Letter]

Name
Address
Phone Number

Date

Addressee
Addressee Title
Company
Address

Dear *Mr./Ms. Addressee* (or *First Name*, if appropriate):

You were recommended to me in view of your firm's recent decision to expand your individual tax preparation services. After a sixteen-year successful track record with the IRS, I am interested in making a career change to the private sector in a similar area.

My work for the past five years has involved providing leadership for our statewide office audit branch of 150 employees and directing their operations through ten subordinate managers. I received a superior performance award for these efforts. These are some highlights:

- Improved tax return selection criteria and exceeded plan by 20%, achieved lowest no-change rate and highest-dollar-per-case yield in the region.

- Conceived and instituted a new system of team management to overcome low morale among employees.

- Established quality and quantity controls for fraud referral program and increased number of referrals from 8% to 15% that went to prosecution.

My educational background includes a B.S. in Accounting with additional work in Finance. With these experiences, my results orientation, and my commitment to add value, I know that I can be effective in helping you establish an individual tax preparation program.

I would like to discuss this possibility and will phone you later in the week to see if we might get together for a brief exploratory meeting.

Sincerely,

[B. *Target Marketing Letter*]

Name
Address
Phone Number

Date

Addressee
Addressee Title
Company
Address

Dear *Mr./Ms. Addressee* (or *First Name*, if appropriate):

A recent *Wall Street Journal* article stated, "Fully 65% of top management expect Human Resources executives to become more heavily involved in developing policies and strategies in years ahead." The need is there; the trend will increase.

Seeking out and retaining that kind of expertise, however, is difficult. I represent that caliber of Human Resource Management professional. My work experience has been gained through increasing responsibilities with Fortune 500 firms. My colleagues consider me to be a person of intelligence with excellent leadership skills.

I am seeking to associate with a firm interested in combining creative Human Resource Management with top management planning and business strategy. Representative accomplishments include the following:

- Created a state-of-the-art strategic planning process that reduced the cost per hire by 5%, reduced turnover by 18% and increased ROI for training by 45% over the past 15 months.

- Improved the company's EEO position by conducting an innovative cross-cultural training program for managers resulting in a 12% decline in EEO complaints.

- Developed a career-planning process that received coverage in the national magazine, "*Industry Week*" and in AMA's "*Management in Process*" newsletter

- Created an Educational Assistance Program that coordinated with government benefits to provide maximum utilization at the lowest possible cost.

There is considerably more to discuss concerning my professional skills. I would appreciate the opportunity to exchange thoughts with you. I will call you in a few days to arrange an appointment at a mutually convenient time.

Sincerely,

Enclosure

[B. *Target Marketing Letter*]

Name
Address
Phone Number

Date

Addressee
Addressee Title
Company
Address

Dear *Mr./Ms. Addressee* (or *First Name*, if appropriate):

As a skilled product manager with ten years experience at leading consumer products companies, and an avid bicyclist, I feel confident I could make valuable and immediate contributions to Cannondale Bicycle.

- As Product Manager of Earthware Paper Towels, I directed all print advertising, in-store promotions, consumer promotions and local tie-ins, tripling income.

- I reversed Alpine Paperware's lag in the marketplace by implementing an incremental incentive program.

Throughout my career, I have worked closely with sales regarding new product launches and plan promotions. I have hired, developed and motivated staff to produce results.

In addition to my hands-on marketing and sales skills, I offer a key intangible: a heartfelt, lifelong love of bicycling. Last year I rode over 2,000 miles, completed three marathons, helped a dozen friends purchase bicycles, wrote articles for my club's newsletter -- and even did all my own overhauls.

In short, Cannondale is a company where I could combine my marketing and sales skills with my passion for bicycling. I've watched your company grow over the years and I know I could contribute valuable expertise and innovative ideas.

The attached resume provides further information about my background. I will call you in the near future to set up a meeting.

Sincerely,

Enclosure: resume

[B. Target Marketing Letter]

Name
Address
Phone Number

Date

Addressee
Addressee Title
Company
Address

Dear *Mr./Ms. Addressee* (or *First Name*, if appropriate):

Michael Harper, who recently joined your organization in the Accounting area, suggested that I write you directly, expressing my interest in your company. I worked with Michael at NuAge Rentals, and he speaks highly of you and your company's impressive growth.

As a consumer, I watched your rapid expansion and have become a loyal user of your rental service. As an industry leader, it seems to me that there would be many ways to increase incremental profits. These would include:

- Expansion through film sales and processing

- VCR sales and repair

- Increase numbers and frequency of tapes rented

At Michael's suggestion, I am forwarding my resume which highlights additional accomplishments. I will follow-up by telephone to see if we can schedule a mutually convenient meeting to discuss opportunities.

Sincerely,

Enclosure: resume

[C. Search Firm Letter]

Name
Address
Phone Number

Date

Addressee
Addressee Title
Company
Address

Dear *Mr./Ms. Addressee:*

The recent acquisition of First Bank has made me realize that I am ready to pursue a more challenging situation. Louise Lerner of J. L. Simmons and Company suggested I contact you, indicating that you had filled some searches for her in the past and worked on many positions at my level.

My proven track record is in:

- Sales management

- Sales team restructuring and training

- Departmental reorganization

I am eager to apply my sales management accomplishments to the high technology field. Although I prefer to stay in the metropolitan San Francisco-San Jose area, I am open to discussing other career opportunities in the West.

My compensation range includes a base salary in the $60s, supplemented by performance-based bonuses. Your confidentiality is appreciated.

During the day, I can be reached at ( ) ___ - ____.

Sincerely,

Enclosure: resume

[C. Placement Agency letter]

Name
Address
Phone Number

Date

Addressee
Addressee Title
Company
Address

Dear Mr./Ms. Addressee:

Enclosed is a copy of my resume for review against your current assignments in administration supervision/management.

I have an excellent track record in purchasing, cost containment staffing and management. My current compensation is $40,000. I am willing to commute up to an hour for the right position.

During the day, I can be reached at (   ) _____-_____.

Sincerely,

Enclosure

[C. Placement Agency Letter]

Name
Address
Phone Number

Date

Addressee
Addressee Title
Company
Address

Dear Mr./Ms. Addressee:

Enclosed is a resume of my background and experience in production supervision. In my nine years as a supervisor at the Connfield Corporation, my achievements were striking and significant. My income was in the $40K range.

I am now seeking new and challenging responsibilities in an organization with similar needs. If the opportunity were right, I would consider relocation.

I will call next week to arrange a mutually convenient meeting to explore the kinds of assignments that would be appropriate.

Sincerely,

Enclosure

[D. *Open Ad Response Letter with Company Name*]

Name
Address
Phone Number

Date

Addressee
Addressee Title
Company
Address

Dear *Mr./Ms. Addressee:*

Your ad in the National Business Employment Weekly for a Training Director who could expand existing Human Resource Management Programs captured my attention.

For the past twelve years, I have had a proven track record involving all phases of Human Resource Management with major Fortune 500 firms. In my current position, my responsibilities range from organizational training and management development, to EEO/AAP administration, and labor relations.

Some of my accomplishments mentioned in the attached resume are a particular match for your requirements:

- Initiated the development and implementation of Quality Circles and a manufacturing improvement program that increased productivity by 24% within one year.

- Developed and implemented a career assessment, succession planning, and development program oriented to identifying and developing 30 senior and middle-management executives within a two-year period.

- Directed the assessment and design of a divisional management training and development program for 1,400 employees that improved managerial and communications skills.

I would appreciate the opportunity to further explore my background with you. I will contact you next week to arrange a meeting.

Sincerely,

[D. *Open Ad Response Letter with Company Name]*

Name
Address
Phone Number

Date

Addressee
Addressee Title
Company
Address

Dear *Mr./Ms. Addressee:*

I am replying to your advertisement for a Human Resource Generalist with experience in recruiting, benefits, and compensation. From the highlights below and the enclosed resume, you can see that my expertise matches your needs:

Recruiting

- Improved candidate selection ratio from 1-in-15 to 1-in-5 by creating and implementing an interview training program for managers.

- Directed a recruiting campaign that hired 400 specialists and technicians two months ahead of schedule.

Benefits

- Designed a tracking system that reduced short-term disability claims by $215,000 annually.

Compensation

- Formulated a "pay for performance" compensation system that motivated non-exempt employees to greater productivity and enabled supervisors to objectively evaluate performance.

Salary is negotiable based on your job requirements and my related experience. I am looking forward to further discuss how my skills and experience might help the ABC Company meet its Human Resources goals. I will call you next week to arrange an appointment.

Sincerely,

Enclosure

[D. *Ad Response Letter to Blind Ad*]

Name
Address
Phone Number

Date

The Daily News
P.O. Box 42110
New York, NY 10007

Dear Hiring Authority:

Your recent ad for (Position Title) captured my interest. The qualities you seek are well matched to my track record:

Your Needs	**My Qualifications**
Mature, dynamic manager	♦ Fifteen years business experience, six of them as manager.
Experience in Labor	♦ Labor/Management liason; hourly susupervisor
Employee Relations	♦ Quality of Work/Life Focus Groups
	♦ Cost Reduction Program
	♦ Turnover Reduction Program
Communication skills	♦ Made monthly presentations to top management
	♦ Published monthly in-house newsletter
Gets Results	♦ Reduced costs by 12%
	♦ Reduced absenteeism by 18%.
Credentials	♦ B.A., Business Administration

I enclose my resume that covers my experience and qualifications in greater detail.
I would appreciate the opportunity to discuss my credentials in a personal interview.

Sincerely,

Enclosure: resume

[E. Follow-Up Letter after Interview When You Haven't Heard]

Name
Address
Phone Number

Date

Addressee
Addressee Title
Company
Address

Dear *Mr./Ms. Addressee* (or *First Name*, if appropriate):

I am writing to express continued interest in the Assistant Auditor's position I discussed with you and Paulina Simonski on April 21st.

I would welcome the opportunity to further explore the possibilities of my candidacy. If there are any additional questions you'd like to discuss, I'd be happy to meet with you again. I look forward to speaking with you.

Sincerely,

[E. *Follow-Up Letter after Turndown]*

Name
Address
Phone Number

Date

Addressee
Addressee Title
Company
Address

Dear *Mr./Ms. Addressee* (or *First Name*, if appropriate):

Thank you for your July 10 letter advising me of your decision regarding the Director position. I appreciate all the many courtesies you and your staff extended during my visits to your offices.

The position of Director for the Southwest Region is a unique growth opportunity for a well-rounded manager experienced in all aspects of operations, and I sincerely hope the candidate you have selected works out well.

I still believe my qualifications are well suited to the position and to the Southwest organization, and I trust you will keep me in mind as future opportunities arise. I also hope to stay in touch with you personally to discuss trends and activities in the market, since I value your judgment and insight.

Again, thank you for your hospitality. I look forward to talking with you again soon.

Sincerely,

[F. Thank You Letter after Networking Meeting]

Name
Address
Phone Number

Date

Addressee
Addressee Title
Company
Address

Dear *Mr./Ms. Addressee* (or *First Name*, if appropriate):

Thank you for taking the time to talk with me concerning my interest in making a career move. You were a great help to me in seeing areas of potential "fit" in the changing systems environment.

I am currently contacting the people you suggested. Many thanks for offering their names and allowing me to use you as a referral.

Your time and assistance have proved to be very valuable. I'll be sure to let you know how things develop as I move forward with my search.

In the meantime, please let me know if there is any way I can return the favor.

Sincerely,

Enclosure: resume

[G. *Thank You Letter after Interview*]

Name
Address
Phone Number

Date

Addressee
Addressee Title
Company
Address

Dear *Mr./Ms. Addressee* (or *First Name*, if appropriate):

I appreciated the opportunity to meet with you last Wednesday, to discuss the position of Associate Engineer in A & R's Commercial Manufacturing Division. It was interesting to hear about the new contracts you have recently received and the company's long-term goals under its new management.

To answer your question concerning my experience with polymers and plastics more thoroughly, I would point to my accomplishments at Hamilton Oceanographic.

[Note: Cite related achievement with Problem/Action/Result format.]

As agreed, I will call you next week to set up a meeting with Lee Johannsen, Materials Manager. Once again, thank you for your interest in my qualifications.

Sincerely,

[G. Thank You Letter after Meeting Hiring Manager]

Name
Address
Phone Number

Date

Addressee
Addressee Title
Company
Address

Dear *Mr./Ms. Addressee* (or *First Name*, if appropriate):

It was a pleasure meeting with you last Wednesday and learning more about your plans to expand TRS's Information Systems/Graphics unit. I am impressed with your ideas and confident that I can contribute to your objectives.

As I reflected on our discussion, I further considered how my background and accomplishments match your current business and technology needs. Some of the areas where I believe I would have the greatest impact are:

- **Systems Integration**. While at Turner and Evans, I led a Task Force that studied current developments in this area and its implications for the health care industry. As a result of this research, we implemented a system that allowed us to integrate some of our current hardware using software interfaces.

- **Publishing**. My background in publishing can be of great use to your business units. With 12 years of experience in this area I believe I could provide the units with easy-to-use, substantive information in a creative and enjoyable format. This would facilitate both their decision-making as well as their keeping up-to-date on division activities.

If you have further questions, feel free to contact me during business hours or in the evening. I look forward to hearing from you.

Sincerely,

[H. *Detailed Acceptance Letter*]

Name
Address
Phone Number

Date

Addressee
Addressee Title
Company
Address

Dear *Mr./Ms. Addressee* (or *First Name*, if appropriate):

I'd like to thank you for and accept your offer to join Atlas Investments as Manager, Sales & Marketing, reporting directly to you, effective February 15, 199__, at an annual salary of $65,000.

To ensure that we are clear on the other terms and conditions of our agreement, I have summarized my understanding below:

- ▪ The normal 30-day waiting period for health insurance coverage will be waived under Atlas' group plans so that all coverages will be effective for my dependents and me from February 15, 199__.

- ▪ I will be eligible for three weeks vacation in January, 199__, instead of the standard two weeks.

- ▪ You will be handling the sale of my home in the event that I am unable to do so within the next 60 days.

I look forward to working with you and Atlas, and will plan to meet with you on February 15, immediately following the new employee orientation program. In the meantime, please let me know if there is any other information required or other matters we need to discuss prior to my start date.

Best regards,

[Detailed Acceptance Letter]

Name
Address
Phone Number

Date

Addressee
Addressee Title
Company
Address

Dear *First Name*:

I would like to accept and formally thank you for your offer to join Comtex as Accounting Manager, reporting directly to you, effective May 1, 1997, at an annual salary of $75,500.

By way of ensuring that we are clear about the terms and conditions of our agreement, I have summarized my understanding below. Please let me know if we are in disagreement on these points.

- The usual 6 month Performance Review will be reduced to 90 days at which time, assuming that my performance has been satisfactory, my annual salary will be raised to $80,200.

- I will be eligible for three weeks of vacation in 199_ instead of the usual two weeks.

- Comtex will be supplying me with a laptop computer with which I can telecommute at least one day per week.

- Comtex will also provide me with a cellular phone and a beeper.

I look forward to working with you and the Comtex team and will report for orientation on May 1.

Best regards,

[H. *Abbreviated Acceptance Letter*]

Name
Address
Phone Number

Date

Addressee
Addressee Title
Company
Address

Dear *Mr./Ms. Addressee* (or *First Name*, if appropriate):

I am pleased to accept your offer of employment as General Accounting Manager at IWC. The arrangements you outlined in your letter of November 5, 199__ are quite satisfactory.

I am excited about the opportunity to work with you and your staff, and I look forward to joining you on November 15.

Sincerely,

[Note: This letter is applicable when offer conditions have been carefully and completely delineated in writing.]

[1. *Withdrawal from Consideration Letter*]

Name
Address
Phone Number

Date

Addressee
Addressee Title
Company
Address

Dear *Mr./Ms. Addressee* (or *First Name*, if appropriate):

It was a pleasure meeting with you and your staff to discuss your needs for a payroll manager. Our time together was both enjoyable and informative.

After careful consideration, I have decided to withdraw from the selection process in order to accept a position elsewhere.

Thank you for the opportunity to learn more about your facility. You have a fine team, and I am sure that the candidate you do select will enjoy working with each of you.

Best wishes to you and your staff.

Sincerely,

2. SAMPLE NON-CUSTOMIZED LETTERS

[A. *Broadcast Letter*]

Name
Address
Phone Number

Date

Addressee
Addressee Title
Company
Address

Dear *Mr./Ms. Addressee* (or *First Name*, if appropriate):

Many segments of the American economy are shrinking in "real" terms. Among these is the Corporate Relocation Business, which experienced a 17 percent drop in actual home sales due to moves between 1987 and 1990.

During this same time period, however, as Vice President of Sales and Marketing for the Colony Relocation Company, I increased our business base by 26 percent resulting in a $5 million increase in revenues.

I accomplished this by reorganizing our sales and marketing department to focus on more attractive geographic segments and introducing a new performance-based incentive and bonus programs. I bring a strong bottom-line orientation and unique people management skills to a business situation.

Because of the major restructuring taking place in the industry and at Colony, I am considering other career directions. Real estate development is a natural area for me to consider; hence this letter to you.

I would greatly appreciate the opportunity to visit with you to exchange views on developments in this industry. To that end, I will call your office in a few days to arrange an appointment.

I look forward to meeting you.

Sincerely,

[B. *Progress Letter*]

Name
Address
Phone Number

Date

Addressee
Addressee Title
Company
Address

Dear *Mr./Ms. Addressee* (or *First Name*, if appropriate):

I promised to keep you informed about the progress of my job search. While I have not yet found the right opportunity, I am confident that success is just around the corner.

Here is a quick update:

Activity has picked up over the last three months.

Changing industries in this market has proven difficult, because many candidates with industry experience are available.

Relocation is probably necessary; I'm targeting Boston to Atlanta.

I'm also targeting service organizations with a health care focus.

I'm encouraged by the support I continue to receive and the recent activity in the work market. I've fine-tuned my resume, per your suggestions and I've enclosed a copy for review.

Please keep me in mind for any position that you may hear about. Ideally, I'm looking for a company that places a premium on a quality level of customer service as their driving force toward profitability and growth.

Thank you again for your help and support.

Sincerely,

Enclosure: resume

[C. *Announcement of New Position Letter #1]*

Name
Address
Phone Number

Date

Addressee
Addressee Title
Company
Address

Dear *Mr./Ms. Addressee* (or *First Name*, if appropriate):

Thank you for your time and support during my career transition. I'm pleased to announce that I have accepted a position with (Company) as (Title) in Dallas, Texas.

The search for a new position was a rewarding experience for me, not only because of its successful conclusion but also because it presented me with many opportunities to communicate with skilled, knowledgeable people. I appreciate your specific assistance and your willingness to exchange ideas with me during this process.

If there is any way that I can be helpful to you in the future, I would very much welcome the opportunity.

Very truly yours,

[C. Announcement of New Position Letter #2]

Name
Address
Phone Number

Date

Addressee
Addressee Title
Company
Address

Dear *Mr./Ms. Addressee* (or *First Name*, if appropriate):

Thank you for your time and support during my job search campaign. I have recently accepted a position as Manager with Computer Equipment Investors, Inc. in Princeton, New Jersey.

My job search was particularly rewarding, not only in its conclusion but in the opportunity it provided to meet many outstanding people.

If at any time I can be helpful to you, I would welcome the opportunity.

My best regards,

IV.
Negotiating

Table of Contents

Sample Monthly Contractor Agreement

AGREEMENT

THIS AGREEMENT, made this _____ day of _____ between _____, Inc. having its principal office at (Address, City, State, Zip) (hereafter _____) and:

Name of Contractor:

Address of Contractor:

Social Security # or E.I.N.:

Witnesseth:

WHEREAS, _____ (hereafter "Contractor").

has contracted with a client (the "Client") to provide _____ services, and

WHEREAS, Contractor has specialized skills that would be useful to _____ in providing the services required by Clients.

NOW, THEREFORE, the parties do hereby mutually agree as follows:

FIRST: _____ hereby contracts with Contractor and Contractor hereby agrees to perform _____ services required by the Client for a period of _____ month(s), commencing on _____ (the "Contract Period"). During the Contract Period, Contractor will consult with the Client and its designated employees and former employees. This shall be at such times and places as are mutually agreeable between Contractor and the Client, in consultation with _____. Contractor shall use best efforts in providing the services required by Clients.

SECOND: It is specifically understood and agreed that Contractor is an independent contractor with the right to control details of performance and not an employee of _____ for any purpose whatsoever. _____ has entered into this agreement in material part because Contractor is a professional and able to serve the Client without significant direction, supervision or control by _____.

THIRD: _____ will pay Contractor compensation hereunder at a monthly rate of $_____ (the "Monthly Payment") during the Contract period, payable biweekly; provided that such payments need not exceed the Client's payment to _____ in connection with the Contractor's services hereunder. _____ will reimburse Contractor for reasonable expenses, provided that such reimbursements need not exceed the Client's reimbursement to _____ for such expenses. The payments provided for in this paragraph constitute full consideration for all services and the results of all services by Contractor. No other payment will be due Contractor for any reason except as expressly provided above unless agreed to in a written understanding signed by an officer of _____.

FOURTH: Contractor is not required to perform services hereunder during specified hours or to report the hours worked to _____, but shall perform the services at such times as are mutually agreeable between Contractor and the Client in consultation with _____. Contractor shall notify _____ as soon as all services for the Client have been completed.

FIFTH: _____ may furnish Contractor with written materials for the services hereunder. Any supplementary materials furnished by Contractor shall be at Contractor's own expense.

SIXTH: Without the consent of _____, Contractor may employ clerical helpers to assist him or her in performing the services for Clients. Such helpers shall not be contractors or employees of _____ for any purpose whatsoever. Contractor alone shall be responsible for all payments due to such helpers, including reimbursement of expenses (if any), and Contractor assumes all risks associated with the services performed by such helpers. Contractor agrees to hold _____ harmless for any debts, liabilities or payments due for any reason in connection with the performance of services by helpers hired or retained by Contractor pursuant to this provision.

SEVENTH: During the Contract Period, Contractor is free to conduct outside business activities provided that, during the Contract Period, Contractor shall not provide such services for any company or entity that is in competition with _____ and further provided that, during the Contract Period and for a period of one year thereafter, Contractor shall not solicit or perform such services for any Client that was a Client of _____ during the Contract Period. The provisions of this paragraph may be waived by _____ only in writing, and waivers shall not be unreasonably withheld.

EIGHTH: For use in its business operations, _____ has developed valuable and confidential customer lists, procedures, materials and other information and documents, to which contractor may have access during the Contract Period. Upon termination of this agreement, Contractor agrees to return to _____ any materials furnished by _____ during the term of this agreement. Contractor further agrees that he or she will not directly or indirectly use or disclose to anyone (other than an officer of _____) either during the Contract Period or after the termination thereof, any business information, methods, trade secrets, lists of customers, or other confidential information or data obtained by Contractor while under contract with _____.

NINTH: Either party may terminate this Agreement on twenty-one (21) days written notice. This Agreement shall automatically terminate without prior notice should the Client, in its sole judgment after consultation with _____, seek to terminate Contractor's services hereunder.

TENTH: This agreement constitutes the entire understanding between the parties, merging all prior understandings and agreements, and may be modified only by a written instrument signed by both Contractor and an officer of _____.

IN WITNESS WHEREOF, the parties hereto have executed this Agreement as of the date first written above.

CONTRACTOR   **CLIENT COMPANY**

By _____   By_____

Date _____   Date_____

Sample Employment Contract

Dated as of _____, 19____

The following sets forth the agreement by and between _____ ("Employee") and _____, Inc., as to the employment of the Employee by _____, Inc.

1. **Positions and Duties.** _____ shall employ Employee and Employee shall accept employment from _____, during the term of this agreement, upon the terms and subject to the conditions set forth below. Employee's duties shall be subject to the direction and control of _____'s Board of Directors and its President or his or her designee or designees.

2. **Outside Activities.** At all times during the term of this Agreement the Employee shall devote his or her full energies, interest, abilities and productive time to the performance of his or her duties and responsibilities hereunder. Unless Employee obtains the prior written consent of _____, Employee shall not render to others services of any kind for compensation, or directly or indirectly engage in any other business activity or own any interest in any enterprise which is engaged in any business or activity that is similar to that carried on or proposed to be carried on by _____.

3. **Confidentiality Agreements.** The obligations of the Employee and the rights of _____ set forth herein are in addition to those set forth in a certain Employee Confidentiality Agreement annexed hereto, which is being executed by the Employee simultaneously with the execution hereof (the "Confidentiality Agreement").

4. **Representations and Warranties.** Employee represents and warrants to and covenants with _____, that (a) he or she has furnished to _____ a true and correct copy of any agreements with any prior employer in the securities industry and is subject to no contractual or other restriction or obligation which is inconsistent with the execution of this letter agreement, the performance of his or her duties hereunder, any rights of _____ hereunder or under the Confidentiality Agreement, (b) upon information and belief, there are no regulatory, self-regulatory, administrative, civil or criminal matters past or present, affecting the employment of Employee by _____.

5. **Salary.** Employee will receive a salary of no less than _____ for the first year of employment and no less than _____ per year for the second year of employment. Such salary shall be payable in equal periodic installments in accordance with _____'s usual practice, but not less frequently than twice monthly, and shall be subject to such payroll and withholding deductions as may be required by law.

6. **Benefits.** During the term of his or her employment, Employee shall be eligible to participate in, subject to their respective terms, all _____ employee (i) group medical, hospitalization and life insurance plans, (ii) pension and profit-sharing plans, and (iii) other benefit plans or programs. _____ shall pay or reimburse Employee for all out-of-pocket expenses for travel, meals, hotel accommodations and the like reasonably incurred by him or her in accordance with _____'s policies and directives (including any required prior approvals) for such expenses in connection with the performance of _____'s business, each such payment or reimbursement to be made upon submission of a statement documenting such expenses as required by _____. During the term of this letter agreement, Employee shall be entitled to an annual paid

vacation of such period as may be established from time to time by _____ for its managerial employees generally.

7. **Bonus Pool**. Within 90 days after the end of each fiscal year of _____ which ends during the term of this letter agreement, _____ shall establish a Bonus Pool (the "Bonus Pool") for the Employee and other members of the Group (the "Group"). The Bonus Pool shall be allocated by the co-managers of the Group on the basis of performance, but subject to the approval of _____'s Board of Directors. Employee shall receive a guaranteed minimum bonus of _____ for the first year of employment and _____ for the second year of employment.

However, if the Bonus Pool allocable to Employee exceeds the above stated minimum guaranteed bonus, Employee shall receive the greater amount.

Employee's bonus shall be payable as follows:

Date Due	Amount
December 15, _ _ _ _	_____
March 31, _ _ _ _	_____
June 30, _ _ _ _	_____

Subject to paragraphs 8, 9, 10, 11 and 12, payments of the guaranteed bonus shall be made on December 15, _ _ _ _ and within thirty days of every due date thereafter.

Additionally, Employee shall receive _____% of gross revenues generated by the Group.

8. **Term**. The term of this letter agreement shall commence on _____ and shall continue in effect as to Employee until _____ or until such time as terminated as provided in paragraph 9, 10, 11 and 12. For the purposes of this letter any unpaid minimum guaranteed bonus for such year is in the same ratio as the number of calendar days in which Employee is in _____'s employment for such year is to 365 days. Upon termination of this agreement pursuant to paragraph 9 or 10, _____'s sole obligation to Employee shall be to pay all salary and minimum guaranteed bonus accrued by him or her up to the date of such termination. Upon termination of this agreement, Employee's obligations under the Confidentiality Agreement shall survive.

9. **Termination upon Death**. In the event of the death of Employee, the employment of, and this agreement with respect to, such deceased Employee shall be terminated; provided always that _____ shall pay any accrued salary and any accrued guaranteed minimum bonuses as of the date of termination to the legal representative of his or her estate.

10. **Termination for Disability**. _____ may terminate the employment of, and this Agreement with respect to, Employee who becomes disabled, including disability by reason of any emotional or mental disorders, physical diseases or injuries, and as a result of such disability is unable to work on a full-time basis for a continuous period of six months or more or any six months in a twelve-month period. Upon such termination, _____

shall have no further liability to such disabled Employee hereunder, except to pay any accrued salary and accrued guaranteed minimum bonus as of the termination date. Upon such termination, such disabled Employee's obligation to _____ under the Confidentiality Agreement shall survive.

11. **Termination of Cause.** _____ may terminate the employment of, and this agreement with respect to, Employee if (a) such Employee breaches his fiduciary duties to _____ or is guilty of fraud or willful malfeasance, (b) such Employee materially breaches any representation, warranty, covenant or agreement contained in this agreement or fails to perform any of his or her obligations under this agreement or duties assigned to him or her pursuant to his or her agreement within 10 days after _____ has given written notice to such Employee of such failure, (c) if Employee materially misrepresents any statement to _____, (d) such Employee is convicted of a crime involving moral turpitude or a felony, (e) such Employee knowingly commits a material violation of any law, rule, regulation or bylaw of a securities exchange or association or other regulatory or self-regulatory body or agency applicable to or any general policy or directive of _____ communicated in writing to such Employee, (f) such Employee fails to follow reasonable instructions and/or policies of _____'s Board of Directors, or (g) such Employee terminates this Agreement at any time.

Upon termination of this letter agreement pursuant to this paragraph 11, _____'s sole obligation to Employee shall be to pay all accrued salary. However, this shall not affect Employee's vested benefits under paragraph 6.

Upon such termination, Employee's obligation to _____ under the Confidentiality Agreement shall survive.

12. **Termination Other Than for Cause.** _____ retains the right to terminate this agreement and/or Employee's employment for cause as set forth in paragraph 11, and notwithstanding anything to the contrary in this letter agreement, _____ shall have the right to terminate this agreement and/or Employee's employment hereunder at any time for any reason other than for cause. In such event _____ shall pay to Employee all salary as it accrues during the term of the contract, subject however to Employee's obligation to look for and obtain suitable employment. Upon Employee obtaining such employment, _____'s obligation under this Paragraph 12 shall cease. However, Employee's obligation to _____ under the Confidentiality Agreement shall survive.

13. **Review.** On _____ and on each of the two subsequent six month periods thereafter during the term of employment, _____ shall provide Employee with an informal verbal review of the Group's performance. Concurrent with the third semi-annual verbal review of the Group's performance, _____ and Employee shall discuss the potential for Employee's continued employment subsequent to the termination of this Agreement.

14. **Successors and Assigns.** The rights and obligations of _____ hereunder shall inure to the benefit of and shall be binding upon the successors and assigns of _____; provided, however, that _____'s obligations or liabilities hereunder may not be assigned without the prior written approval of Employee, except to an affiliate of _____ (which assignment shall not release _____ from its obligations to Employee hereunder) or to a successor to all or substantially all of _____'s assets, business or stock that agrees to be bound hereby. This letter agreement is personal to the Employee and may not be assigned.

15. **Amendment or Waiver**. This letter agreement may not be amended or modified except by an agreement in writing duly executed by the Chairman or President of _____ and the Employee. The failure of _____, on the one hand, or the Employee, on the other hand, at any time to enforce performance by the other of any provision of this letter agreement shall in no way affect _____'s or the Employee's, as the case may be, rights thereafter to enforce the same, nor shall the waiver by _____, on the one hand, or the Employee, on the other hand, of any breach of any provision hereof be deemed to be a waiver by _____ or the Employee, as the case may be, of any other breach of the same or any other provision hereof.

16. **Arbitration**. Except as set forth in the Confidentiality Agreement, any controversy or claim arising out of or relating to this letter agreement, or the breach hereof, shall be settled by arbitration in accordance with the rules of either the NASD or NYSE then in effect. However, Employee and _____ agree that the panel of arbitrators shall consist solely of arbitrators from the securities industry. Judgment upon the award of the arbitrators may be entered in any court having jurisdiction thereof.

17. **Miscellaneous**. The invalidity or unenforceability of any provision of this letter agreement shall not affect the validity or enforceability of any other provision hereof. This letter agreement shall be constructed, interpreted and enforced in accordance with the laws of the state of New York. This letter agreement contains all of the terms and conditions agreed to by the parties hereto with respect to the subject matter hereof and supersedes all prior agreements, understandings, negotiations and discussions, whether oral or written, of the parties, except those set forth in the Confidentiality Agreement.

Employee's employment and the terms and conditions of such employment shall be contingent upon satisfactory completion of _____'s standard pre-employment screening process.

If the foregoing is satisfactory, please indicate your agreement by executing the enclosed copy of this letter agreement in the appropriate place set forth below.

FOREGOING AGREED TO:

By: _____

Title   Employee

By: _____

Title   Name   Employer

Sample Letter of Agreement

LETTER OF AGREEMENT

Between (Supplier)_____ and _____(Customer)

Dated: _____

This Work Order is an Agreement that the Company will perform the professional services outlined in Paragraph 2 (Scope of Work) below, in return for the compensation described inn paragraph 3 (Compensation) below. Such performance is subject to all the terms and conditions listed below.

1. **TERM:** The term of this Agreement shall begin the first day following the acceptance of this letter by (Customer name), and shall expire upon completion of the tasks or hours worked as outlined in the Scope of Work section below.

2. **SCOPE OF WORK:** The professional services and deliverables to be performed by the Supplier are identified below, and if necessary, on the pages which are affixed to this Work Order.

Task/Assignment description _____
Start Date: _____
Customer Address: _____
Phone:_____ E-mail_____
Contact Person: _____
Service Delivery Location: _____

3. **COMPENSATION/REIMBURSEMENT:**

3.1 This Agreement is for (Choose one)
    a. Fixed price of: $_____ per hour/day/month.
    b. Flat fee of $_____
    c. (Other arrangement) $_____

3.2 Cancellation by customer within 15 days of delivery negates this contract but guarantees the payment of
    a. 20% of agreed to fees
    b. Actual expense generated and documented with receipts by the Supplier.

4. **EXPENSES:**   (Customer), hereby authorizes the following expenses for this Agreement, and agrees to reimburse the Supplier for them within 30 days after receiving receipts.

TYPE:
Airfare - Coach/Economy Class
Meals - Reasonable expenses for instructor only
Lodging - Reasonable rates
Miscellaneous -ground transportation, baggage handling, reasonable tips

5. ENTIRE AGREEMENT: This instrument constitutes the entire Agreement of the parties relating to the subject matter hereof and shall supersede any prior oral or written agreements or understanding relating to this Letter of Agreement.

_____   _____

Customer Approval   (Company/Supplier name) Approval

_____   _____

Title   Title

_____   _____

Date   Date

V.
Campaign Action Plan
What To Do If Your Search Stalls

Recordkeeping Forms

Table of Contents

WEEKLY ACTION PLAN (Item #12-1)

Check off as you complete ✔
(Or rate your performance)

NAME _____

WEEK BEGINNING _____

	Networking Activities:							Research:		Interviews/Follow-up:	
	☎ Phone Calls ☎		✉ Letters ✉ Thank You Notes		☺ Meetings ☺			💾💻📁📄			
	Name ▽	✓	Name ▽	✓	Name ▽	✓		Name ▽	✓	Name ▽	✓
Monday Date ☐											
Tuesday Date ☐											
Wednesday Date ☐											
Thursday Date ☐											
Friday Date ☐											

NETWORKING CONTACT RECORD (ITEM #12-2A)
INDEX CARD FORMAT

Here is an example of a good tracking method for your networking contacts -- using index cards.

Name	Office Phone/Fax	Home
Company	**Possible type of Assistance**	
Address	☐ Industry Info. ☐ Intro. to Target ☐ Target Co. Info. ☐ Job Lead ☐ Second Contacts ☐ Feedback ☐ Future References	

Contact	Mode	What Happened?	Follow-up
	☐ Phone ☐ Letter ☐ Interview		☐ Required ☐ Completed
(List referral on back of card)		Referred by	

You can file these alphabetically by individual or company name in a card file and flag those requiring further action. You can take them with you to appointments/meetings. Be sure to cross-index them to your correspondence.

FULL PAGE/NOTEBOOK FORMAT
NETWORKING CONTACT RECORD (Item #12-2B)

CONTACT NAME	Follow-up Date: _____	REFERRED BY:
	Status: _____	Contact Name:

Title/Function:

Business Phone #:   Title/Function:

Business Fax #:

Company Name: Company Name:

Street Address:

City/State/Zip:

Background Information On Contact

Relationship to referring person:

Family: spouse, children, pets:

Age:

Hobbies:

Interests:

Other:

Date	STATUS/COMMENTS:

INTERVIEW LOGSHEET (Item #12-3)

F I L L   O U T   P R I O R   T O   I N T E R V I E W

Name:	Phone #: Fax

Title:	Interview Date:

Company Name:

Address:

Background Information on

Information on Company:
- Scope of Work
- Compensation Package
- Names & Titles of Key People
- Organizational Structure
- Key Locations
- Products/Services/Lines of Business

Desired Outcome/Next Step:

A F T E R   I N T E R V I E W

What Worked Well:

Areas for Improvement:

Reactions to/from Others:

Main Interests in My Background:

What Happens Next (What, Who, When):

CORRESPONDENCE LOGSHEET ITEM (#12-4)

Type of Correspondence	Name/Address/Phone/Fax	Mail Date	Phone Date		Result of Follow-up	Written Reply Rec'd	Further Action
			Sched'd	Actual			

ADVERTISEMENT RECORD (ITEM #12-5)

THE AD: Appeared in: _____

(Publication)

_____   _____

(Edition)   (Date)

_____ Sent attached letter with _____ attached

_____ Phoned number given, spoke to _____

■   Result:

■   Follow up required:

_____ Researched/networked for more information on company

_____ Plan to follow up by _____

with _____

Notes from research:

_____

_____

_____

_____

_____

VI.
Bibliography

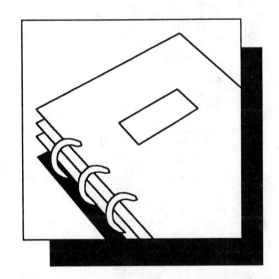

Bibliography

Time Management

Alexander, Roy. *Common Sense Time Management*. Amacom, 1992.

Allen, Jane Elizabeth. *Beyond Time Management*. Addison-Wesley, 1986.

Barnes, Emilie. *The Fifteen Minute Organizer*. Harvest House, 1991.

Covey, Stephen R. *First Things First*. Simon & Schuster, 1989.

Douglass, Donna M. and Merrill E. Douglass. *Manage Your Time, Manage Your Work, Manage Yourself*. Amacom, 1980.

Drucker, Peter. *The Effective Executive*. Harper and Row, 1967.

Hunt, Diana and Pam Hait. *The Tao of Time*. Simon & Schuster, 1990.

Josephs, Ray. *How to Gain an Extra Hour Every Day*. Plume, 1992.

Kanarek, Lisa. *Organizing your Home Office for Success*. Plume, 1993.

Lakein, Alan. *How to Get Control of Your Time and Your Life*. Peter Wyden, 1973.

Levinson, Jay Conrad. *The Ninety Minute Hour*. Dutton, 1990.

McGee-Cooper, Ann. *Time Management for Unmanageable People*. Bowen & Rogers/Self, 1993.

McGee-Cooper, Ann. *You Don't Have to Go Home From Work Exhausted*. Bantam, 1990.

McNally, David. *Even Eagles Need A Push*. Transform Press, 1990.

Salzman, Amy. *Downshifting*. Harper Perennial, 1992.

Smith, Hyrum W. *The 10 Natural Laws of Successful Time and Life Management: Proven Strategies for Increased Productivity and Inner Peace*. `Warner Books, 1994.

Winston, Stephanie. *Stephanie Winston's Best Organizing Tips*. Simon & Schuster, 1995.

Bibliography

CAREER MANAGEMENT

Armstrong, Howard. *High Impact Telephone Networking for Job Hunters.* Bob Adams, 1992.

Bolles, Richard. *The Three Boxes of Life, and How to Get Out of Them.* Ten Speed Press, 1981.

Bolles, Richard. *What Color is Your Parachute*? Ten Speed Press (updated annually).

Bridges, William. *JobShift.* Addison-Wesley, 1994.

Bridges, William. *Transitions: Making Sense of Life's Changes.* Addison-Wesley, 1980.

Cohen, H. *You Can Negotiate Anything.* Lyle Stewart, 1980.

Covey, Stephen. *The 7 Habits of Highly Effective People.* Simon and Schuster, 1989.

Gray, Terry. How to Search the Web: A Guide to Search Tools, http:/daphne.palomar.edu/TGSEARCH/

Handy, Charles. *The Age of Paradox.* Harvard Business School Press, 1994.

Handy, Charles. *The Age of Unreason.* Harvard Business School Press, 1989.

Hyatt, Carole. *Shifting Gears.* Simon and Schuster, 1990.

Kanter, Rosabeth Moss. *When Giants Learn to Dance: Mastering the Challenge of Strategy, Management, and Careers in the 1990s.* Simon and Schuster, 1989.

Land, George & Jarman, Beth. *Breakpoint and Beyond: Mastering the Future — Today.* Haraber Business, 1992.

Myers, Isabel Briggs with Peter B. Myers. *Gifts Differing.* Consulting Psychologists Press, 1980.

Pritchett, Price. *New Work Habits for a Radically Changing World.* Pritchett & Associates, 1994.

Sacharov, Al. *Offbeat Careers.* Ten Speed Press, 1988.

Seligman, Martin. *Learned Optimism.* Pocket Books, Simon and Schuster, 1990.

Seuss, Dr. *Oh, The Places You'll Go.* Random House, 1990.

Sher, Barbara. *Wishcraft.* Ballantine, 1979.

Sinetar, Marsha. *Do What You Love and the Money Will Follow.* Paulist Press, 1987.

Tieger, Paul D. and Barbara Barron-Tieger. *Do What You Are.* Little, Brown, 1993.

Bibliography

HEALTH

Arnot, Dr. Robert. *Dr. Bob Arnot's Guide to Turning Back the Clock*. Little, Brown & Company, 1995.

Bailey, Covert. *Smart Exercise*. Houghton, Mifflin, 1994.

Bailey, Covert. *Smart Eating*. Houghton Mifflin, 1994.

Chopra, Deepak. *Ageless Body, Timeless Mind*. Harmony Books, 1993.

Chopra, Deepak. *Creating Health*. Houghton Mifflin, 1987.

Chopra, Deepak. *Perfect Health*. Harmony Books, 1990.

Chopra, Deepak. *Quantum Healing*. Bantam Books, 1989.

Cooper, Kenneth. *Health and Fitness Excellence*. Houghton Mifflin, 1989.

Dimond, Harvey and Marilyn Dimond. *Fit for Life*. Warner Books, 1985.

Dimond, Harvey and Marilyn Dimond. *Fit for Life II*. Warner Books, 1987.

Heller, Dr. Richard F. and Dr. Rachel F. Heller. *Healthy for Life*. Penguin Books, 1996.

Pinckney, Callan. *Callanetics*. G.P. Putnam's Sons, 1995.

Powter, Susan. *Food*. Simon & Schuster, 1995.

Bibliography

STRESS MANAGEMENT

Benson, Dr. Herbert. *The Relaxation Response.* Wings Books, 1992.

Gawain, Shakti. *Creative Visualization.* New World Library, 1978.

Frisher, Dion. *44 Easy Ways to Relieve Stress.* Arborvitae Publications, 1994.

Hanson, Dr. Peter. *The Joy of Stress.* Universal Press, 1985.

Matheny, Kenneth B. *Stress and Strategies for Lifestyle Management.* Georgia State University Business Press, 1992.

Moskowitz, Reed C. *Your Healing Mind.* William Morrow, 1992.

Nathan, Ronald G., et al. *The Doctor's Guide to Instant Stress Relief.* Ballantine, 1989.

Sapolsky, Robert W. *Why Zebras Don't Get Ulcers: A Guide to Stress, Stress-Related Diseases, and Coping.* W. H. Freeman, 1994.

Seligman, Martin E. P. *Learned Optimism.* Pocket Books, 1990.

Smith, Jonathan C. *Understanding Stress and Coping.* MacMillan, 1993.

Notes

Notes

Notes

Notes

Notes

Notes

Notes

Notes

Notes

Notes